MIKHAIL BULGAKOV

Born in Kiev in 1891, where he studied and briefly practised medicine before settling in Moscow in 1921, Bulgakov sprang to notice as a writer in 1925 with the publication of *The White Guard*, his novel about the Soviet Civil War. The Moscow Art Theatre under Stanislavsky commissioned a dramatisation, which was staged the following year. Its sympathetic portrayal of the 'White' enemy brought Bulgakov official disapproval, which intensified following his satiric comedy, *Zoia's Apartment*, for the Vakhtangov Theatre (1926) and *The Crimson Island*, for Taïrov's Kamerny Theatre (1927). In 1929 all his plays were banned, so that much of his subsequent work for the theatre was not published or performed in his lifetime. This was the case with *Flight*, written in 1927 but not staged until 1957, and with such plays as *Adam and Eve*, *Bliss* and *Ivan Vassilievich*. However his adaptation of Gogol's *Dead Souls* was staged at the Moscow Art Theatre in the thirties, as was his play about Molière, with whom he felt a great affinity, writing his biography in 1933. Bulgakov satirised his relationship with Stanislavsky in the novel, *Black Snow* (1936, published in 1965), but his prose masterpiece is *The Master and Margarita*, completed at his death in 1940, first published in 1967 and triumphantly staged by Lyubimov at the Taganka in 1977.

RON HUTCHINSON

Born in Northern Ireland, brought up in Coventry, Ron Hutchinson has won both the George Devine and the John Whiting Awards for his stage plays, which include *Says I, Says He* (1977), *The Irish Play* (1980) and *Rat in the Skull* (1984), first staged by the Royal Court Theatre and revived there in 1996. Since 1986 he has lived in Los Angeles, where he writes for television and film. His work has received multiple Emmy and Golden Globe Awards.

D0863208

Other Titles in this Series

MIKHAIL BULGAKOV

Flight

adapted by

Ron Hutchinson

ROYAL NATIONAL THEATRE

LONDON

NICK HERN BOOKS

LONDON

A Nick Hern Book

Flight first published in Great Britain in this version
as an original paperback in 1998 jointly by the
Royal National Theatre, London, and Nick Hern Books Limited,
14 Larden Road, London W3 7ST

The text printed here is the version prepared by Ron Hutchinson
for the National Theatre production, but changes may have taken
place in rehearsal which have not been incorporated into the
printed edition

Typeset by Country Setting, Woodchurch, Kent TN26 3TB
Printed in England by Cox and Wyman Ltd, Reading, Berks

ISBN 1 85459 379 X

A CIP catalogue record for this book is available from
the British Library

This adaptation of *Flight* was first staged in the Olivier auditorium of the Royal National Theatre, London. First preview was 5 February 1998; press night was 12 February. The cast was as follows:

SERGEI GOLUBKOV	Michael Mueller
MONK	Christopher Campbell
ARCHBISHOP ATHANASIUS	Collin Johnson
COMRADE COMMANDER BAYEV	Jean-Benoit Blanc
MAJOR GENERAL GRISHA CHARNOTA	Kenneth Cranham
SOLDIER	John Webber
DE BRISARD	Iain Mitchell
LYUSKA	Rachel Power
KRAPILIN	Richard O'Callaghan
SERAFIMA KORZUKHIN	Abigail Cruttenden
ROMAN KHLUDOV	Alan Howard
STAFF OFFICERS	Paul Blair, Peter Bygott,
	Christopher Campbell, Simon Coleman
	Isaac Maxwell-Hunt, John Webber, John Dorney
STATIONMASTER	Benny Young
CAPTAIN GOLOVAN	Louis Hilyer
OLGA	Kylie Tuffney, Chloe White
PARAMON KORZUKHIN	Nicholas Jones
COMMANDER IN CHIEF OF THE WHITE ARMY	Peter Blythe
TIKHI	Geoffrey Hutchings
SKUNSKY	Mark Bonnar
ORDERLIES Guy Manning, Peter Bygott, Christopher Campbell
TURKISH WOMAN	Emma Poole
BRITISH SAILOR	John Webber
YANKO YANKOVICH	Iain Mitchell
AMOROUS GREEK	Paul Blair
REFUGEES, SOLDIERS, MONKS, CLERKS,	
INTERROGATERS, LOOTERS, TURKS	
	Joscelyn Best, Natasha Joseph, Rebecca Lenkiewicz

Director Howard Davies
Settings Tim Hatley
Lighting Rick Fisher
Music Paddy Cunneen
Director of Movement Jane Gibson
Company Voice Work Patsy Rodenburg
Sound Paul Groothuis

Characters

SERAFIMA KORZUHKIN, *a young woman from St. Petersburg*

SERGEI GOLUBKOV, *a University Professor from St. Petersburg*

ARCHBISHOP ATHANASIUS,
   alias MAKHROV

MADAME BARABANCHIKOVA,
   alias MAJOR GENERAL CHARNOTA

COMRADE COMMANDER BAYEV, *Red Cavalry officer*

LYUSKA, *Charnota's lover*

KRAPILIN, *Charnota's Orderly*

DE BRISARD, *Commander of a White Hussar Regiment*

COMMANDER IN CHIEF *of the White Army*

ROMAN KHLUDOV, *White Chief of Staff*

CAPTAIN GOLOVAN, *Aide to Khludov*

STATIONMASTER

OLGA, *the Stationmaster's nine-year-old daughter*

PARAMON KORZUKHIN, *errant husband of Serafima*

TIKHI, *Chief of White Counter-Intelligence*

SKUNSKY, *White Counter-Intelligence Officer*

YANKO YANKOVICH, *Cockroach King of Constantinople*

GIRL CASHIER, *Assistant to Yanko*

FAT TURKISH WOMAN

AMOROUS GREEK

TURKISH PORTER

ORDERLIES

First Dream

The sound of a steam train gets louder and louder, its whistle sounding shrilly in the dark. A mass of confused and frightened REFUGEES *rushes on, pushing handcarts with all their possessions on them, or piled on their backs.*

The train whistles again, there's the sound of explosions and sudden flashes of artillery fire as another group of equally desperate REFUGEES *rushes on from the opposite direction.*

A bell tolls frantically as the two groups mix like two streams rushing together, eddy, swirl, break apart, scurry in different directions as the train whistles again and more explosions sound.

Among them, pushing a handcart in which the pregnant BARABANCHIKOVA *is lying, is* GOLUBKOV. *With some of the other refugees he flees into a dimly lit monastery, inside whose walls lie the old, the sick and the frightened.*

It's suddenly very quiet save for the distant chanting of MONKS *as he gives voice to his agony of indecision –*

GOLUBKOV. The Urals, yes, that's the place to aim for –

Two steps in one direction and he hesitates.

Or perhaps back to St. Petersburg, things have probably sorted themselves out there by now –

Two steps in a different direction and another hesitation.

No, that's ridiculous, they won't be sorted out for a hundred years –

He sets the heavy handcart and its burden down and winces apologetically as the passenger on it gives a gasp.

I'm sorry, Madame, I really do have to rest for a moment.

As she groans again he hastily searches for something for her to eat and drink.

There's some bread and a little cheese left and this is the last of the water – help yourself –

The wavering hand reaches for it and he reluctantly surrenders it, watching as it's all swiftly devoured.

What a terrible thing to bring a baby into the world like this. What if there are complications? I suppose what I should do is go to the village and find a doctor or a midwife for you.

I'll go right away.

The sound of distant artillery makes him hesitate.

Should I go? I'll go. It can't be far. If that's artillery it means they're still some distance away.

Another hesitation.

Or are they getting nearer? But what if they are? To be hit by an artillery shell, to be standing just where it lands, the odds against that happening to you, to be on the exact spot where one particular shell is heading, those odds must be pretty high, don't you think?

Paralysed by his too familiar indecision.

Excuse the impertinence, Madame, but when can we expect the happy event? Just so that I can weigh the alternatives, make a rational decision –

Before MADAME BARABANCHIKOVA *can answer a trap door opens in the floor and a* MONK *pops his head out.*

MONK. Get your papers out! Here they come!

GOLUBKOV. Who? Who's coming? The Reds or the Whites?

The terrified MONK *disappears again as the refugees frantically pull out their sets of false papers. One of them starts to shake in an extremis of fear as he sees the interlopers approach.*

MAKHROV. Buggering shit. Fuck. Bugger bugger bugger. Sod it. We're fucked. The Reds.

The burly Red Army soldier BAYEV *rushes on, flanked by* SOLDIERS *who surround the refugees, guns at the ready.*

BAYEV. Right, you lot, who's been signalling to the Whites? You think I'm stupid? You think I don't know why those bells are being rung? (*Snapping orders to his escort.*) Get up the belfry and see who's flashing that light. We'll sort the bastards out.

Some of his escort heads away and the papers in the refugees' hands flutter as they shakily hold them out.

Who wants to see some monks being shot, eh? Hands up. We're going to have a massacre here, we're going to shoot this entire monkey house of monks.

We're going to line them all up from the Abbot himself down to the littlest bum boy in the choir and we're going to spatter them all over the walls –

He swaggers towards MAKHROV, GOLUBKOV *and the cart.*

After that, know what we're going to do? We're going to have another massacre, a mini massacre of everyone who's been helping them. Men, women, children, the more the merrier, do I look as if I give a shit?

(*To* MAKHROV.) Who are you?

MAKHROV. I'm a chemist from Kiev.

BAYEV. I'm a massacrer from Mariupul, tough luck. Papers.

He takes the papers MAKHROV *holds out with a trembling hand.*

MAKHROV. I was in the market buying some cucumbers, I only slipped out for ten minutes and then, bang, shells started falling and I never did get the cucumbers.

BAYEV. Shut your gob.

He pushes the papers back at him, turns to GOLUBKOV.

What's your reason for being so near the front line?

GOLUBKOV. It's so very hard to know where that line is, Comrade. It changes every day. It's like a balloon tied to you on a piece of string, wherever you go it's there, bumping into you.

BAYEV. Nancy boy, are you?

GOLUBKOV. No, Comrade –

BAYEV. You sound like one.

Shots sound offstage and GOLUBKOV *tries to keep his voice steady as he indicates the cart.*

GOLUBKOV. This lady is going to have a baby at any moment. They threw everybody off the train and left us here.

BAYEV. What's your name?

BARABANCHIKOVA (*in a weak fluting voice*). Bara – Barabanchikova, comrade –

BAYEV. Don't you bloody comrade me. Papers.

He disregards more shots as he inspects the papers she gives him with a trembling hand.

Where's the old man then?

BARABANCHIKOVA. Sergei Pavlovich is – oh it's terrible, too terrible –

She bursts into sobs but BAYEV *isn't impressed. He puts his ear to the swollen belly.*

BAYEV. Whose little bastard are you, eh?

BARABANCHIKOVA. Comrade, please, I beg you –

BAYEV. I have to tell you I find it highly suspicious that your first impulse on knowing you was to drop one was to head for a monastery.

A dangerous look at GOLUBKOV *and the others.*

In fact, I find that highly significant all around.

The menace in his voice causes his soldiers to raise their weapons, aiming them at GOLUBKOV *and the others.*

All right, boys. Sleeping beauty first.

GOLUBKOV. You can't shoot her –

He steps towards BAYEV *and a half dozen guns are pointed directly at him.*

BAYEV. Why not?

GOLUBKOV. She's – well – because of her condition.

BAYEV. Up the spout? I think it's tasty that, I think it's got style, starting off massacring a pregnant woman.

The breathless execution party rush back, carrying rifles.

SOLDIER. Time to go, Comrade Commander.

BAYEV. We haven't killed any of this lot yet –

SOLDIER. It'll have to keep. There's more troops heading this way and I don't think they're ours.

BAYEV. Always the bloody way, always the bloody same. You're just about to get some work done and some counter revolutionary arsehole finds a way to louse it up –

Shots sound, too close for comfort. With a final look around at his cowering, would be victims –

BAYEV. We'll be back, boys and girls. You're going nowhere. Especially you –

On impulse he sticks the gun against GOLUBKOV*'s head, grinning.*

Why shouldn't I do it?

GOLUBKOV. That's something I should be the last person to ask.

A moment's hesitation, then BAYEV *lowers the gun. He heads away with the soldiers, and* GOLUBKOV, MAKHROV *and the refugees suck in air, thankful at their narrow escape.*

The strangest thing – as he was holding that gun to my head something popped into my mind. It was the green lampshade on the desk in my study back home in St. Petersburg.

It's very odd. I can hardly remember the faces of any of my friends – dead, exiled, imprisoned – but I saw that green lampshade as clearly as if I could reach out and touch it –

What were the Reds doing here, anyway? We were told the Whites would never surrender a yard of territory in the Ukraine. How did it happen?

BARABANCHIKOVA. It happened because General Krapchikov is too fond of whist –

She raises herself on her elbow.

With some men it's drink or women. With Krapchikov it's cards –

Anger makes the voice thicker and lower.

He'd rather play cards than do anything else, such as read the Intelligence reports that would have told him exactly where and when the Red Guards were going to attack –

She coughs and her voice resumes its fluting quality.

That's why we're in this mess.

MAKHROV. You seem to know a tremendous amount about conditions at Headquarters, Madame.

The voice sounds lower and angrier again.

BARABANCHIKOVA. Leave me alone the lot of you. God how boring all this is.

A clatter of hoofbeats muffled shouts and curses, flashing lanterns as dark figures approach, scattering the refugees on either side.

MAKHROV. Fuck and faeces, what now?

GOLUBKOV. It's all right, those are Whites, the officers are wearing epaulets –

MAKHROV (*mocking*). 'It's all right, the officers have epaulets.' What's to stop the Reds disguising themselves as ours?

GOLUBKOV. I never thought of that. It would hardly be fair.

MAKHROV. You bloody St. Petersburg intellectuals –

GOLUBKOV (*staring off stage*). My God, you're right, they're wearing red breeches –

MAKHROV. They're blue breeches with red down the sides –

GOLUBKOV. Are you sure?

MAKHROV. Or else they're red breeches with blue stripes –

BARABANCHIKOVA. For Christ's sake, get me off this damn thing and let me take a look –

'Madame Barabanchikova' jumps off the cart revealing himself to be a man – GENERAL CHARNOTA. *He's brisk, efficient, cultured, with the generally unflustered air of a man of action.*

CHARNOTA. Thank God for that. Don Cossacks. We're safe.

He pulls the cloak off, revealing a White Army uniform.

Congratulations, Golubkov. You must have hit every bump in the road between here and the railway station.

GOLUBKOV. Who are you?

CHARNOTA. Does that matter?

A platoon of WHITE SOLDIERS *rushes on, led by* COLONEL DE BRISARD, *who's followed by the private* KRAPILIN. *Briskly efficient,* DE BRISARD *starts giving orders.*

DE BRISARD. Against the wall please, everyone. Men, women, children. That's the way, let's get this over with –

MAKHROV (*despairing*). Not another madman –

CHARNOTA. Is this really necessary, de Brisard?

DE BRISARD. My God – General Charnota.

LYUSKA *rushes on and throws herself at* CHARNOTA.

LYUSKA. Grisha –

CHARNOTA. Lyuska –

LYUSKA. I thought I'd never see you again –

CHARNOTA. That damn fool Krapchikov tried to make sure of that. He insisted on a final hand of whist. Halfway through the lights went out and there they were. I had to shoot my way out – me, a General – and stick my pistol in the ear of the first person I met for his papers. Unfortunately, in the rush he gave me his wife's instead plus a certificate saying she had to get extra rations due to her – condition, as you call it.

GOLUBKOV. You might have told me who you were.

CHARNOTA. Come now, Golubkov, you can't deny the warm glow of pleasure you got from helping me.

The impatient LYUSKA *throws herself at* CHARNOTA *again.*

LYUSKA. We've been fighting non stop for weeks. Holding a village here, retreating there. Reprisals, hostages, raiding parties, you know what it's like. I feel like we've crossed half of Russia and back.

CHARNOTA. Where's Krapchikov?

LYUSKA. He's at Headquarters. Wherever Headquarters is.

CHARNOTA. Come with me, Lyuska. I have an urgent desire to catch General Krapchikov before the Reds do and shoot him myself.

He exits with LYUSKA, *leaving the others at the mercy of* DE BRISARD, *who's humming agitatedly under his breath.*

DE BRISARD. Please get in line, everyone, we don't have all day. The Reds were here minutes ago. There's no smoke without fire –

KRAPILIN *raises his rifle and shoots and* GOLUBKOV *and the refugees dive for cover as the bullets fly wildly around, thankfully without hitting anyone.*

What are you doing?

KRAPILIN. You said fire, Your Excellency.

DE BRISARD. Wait for the order, Krapilin, we're a military unit, not bank robbers. (*Sighs.*)

Now that you've started you may as well finish – but I swear to God, as soon as I can get rid of you, I shall.

Well – what are you waiting for now?

As he swings his gun at them MAKHROV *falls on his knees, pulls his hat off, revealing himself to be* ARCHBISHOP ATHANASIUS.

MAKHROV. You can't shoot me. I'm an Archbishop. Archbishop Athanasius.

The gun swings towards GOLUBKOV.

DE BRISARD. You're his Altar Boy, I suppose.

GOLUBKOV. I'm Sergei Golubkov. I'm a University student. My father is one of the most distinguished professors of philosophy in Russia. Conditions in St. Petersburg are totally impossible. I made the decision to offer my services to the Whites.

DE BRISARD. Quite sure of the colour?

GOLUBKOV. Quite.

DE BRISARD. Somebody has to be shot. How would it look if we let you all go?

Before KRAPILIN *can open fire* CHARNOTA *rushes back in with* LYUSKA.

CHARNOTA. No time for that now, De Brisard. The Reds are outflanking us again.

Staring down with contempt at MAKHROV.

I suggest you put your skids on, Athanasius. If the Reds catch you you'll be able to preach about the crucifixion from personal experience.

Sobbing in terror, ATHANASIUS *rushes out.*

DE BRISARD. Is the other one who he says he is, too?

CHARNOTA *looks directly at* GOLUBKOV, *shrugs.*

CHARNOTA. How would I know? (*To* KRAPILIN.) Give me the map.

KRAPILIN. Sir –

CHARNOTA. This won't be as much fun as terrorizing civilians, De Brisard, but there's a chance we might be able to link up with General Khludov in the Crimea if we move fast enough.

Peering at the map that KRAPILIN *hands him.*

I want you to head in close order for Babii Gai, pull the Reds after you, disengage here, double back here and ford the river here, even if you have to swim for it. I'll bring any troops I can find in a wide sweep north as if I'm heading for the Dukhobors but I'll wheel south west at the last minute and meet you at Arabat.

DE BRISARD. You think it'll work?

CHARNOTA. No, but it sounds appropriately military and all we have left now are appearances, haven't we?

A final word of advice for GOLUBKOV.

You really should think twice before you act on your philanthropic impulses in the middle of a Civil War. It only confuses things.

He heads out with DE BRISARD, LYUSKA *and* KRAPILIN *as explosions sound, getting closer and closer. Smoke drifts in as the other refugees flee, leaving* GOLUBKOV *feeling very much abandoned and on his own. A voice sounds behind him.*

SERAFIMA. Help me – help me, please –

Turning he sees what looks like a vision – a beautiful young woman illuminated by a shaft of golden light, like an icon of the Virgin.

GOLUBKOV. No – no – this is too much –

Spellbound, he stares at the apparition, trying to resist the temptation of falling on his knees in front of it.

SERAFIMA. Where – where are we? What's the name of this place? How far away is St. Petersburg?

He approaches her carefully, as if she's some kind of religious hallucination.

GOLUBKOV. I'm a refugee and I have no idea where we are –

Pulling back, he approaches her from the other side, wanting to make sure she's there in three dimensions.

GOLUBKOV. I'm a student. I was trying to return my library books and as I passed the railway station I got caught up in a crowd, thousands of people all headed in the same direction and the next thing I knew I was on a train steaming out.

She moves and he jumps back, startled.

SERAFIMA. My husband is Deputy Minister for Trade. I'm trying to reach him. He's somewhere in the Crimea, I think.

GOLUBKOV (*suddenly sceptical*). Really? He's Deputy Minister for Trade? It's amazing the people you run into in a Civil War.

SERAFIMA. He's on a secret mission to General Khludov.

GOLUBKOV. I suppose he would be. Disguised as an Archbishop or something?

SERAFIMA. You don't – you don't believe me?

GOLUBKOV. Pregnant, are you? How many months are you gone? Twins, due at any time?

SERAFIMA. I've only been out of the convent school three months.

GOLUBKOV. I would like to help you, Madame, but in times like these, well, it only confuses things, and they're confused enough already.

You try to help someone and what happens? You make a fool of yourself and the people you help only seem to resent it. It's just so much better for everyone if –

She sways again and her legs give way and he rushes forward and catches her as she falls.

I'm not taken in for a moment –

SERAFIMA. Paramon –

The bell starts to toll frantically again as the trap door opens at their feet and MONKS *start clambering out. Others rush on from the sides.*

GOLUBKOV. This lady says she's the wife of the Deputy Minister for Trade. Perhaps you'd be so good as to take care of her –

The MONKS *ignore him. They tear their vestments off, grab the icons from the walls, stuff them under their civilian clothes and scurry away.*

This lady – excuse me – I have to leave this lady here with you –

It's no use. They've all gone and he's alone with her in the shell of the monastery. A train whistle shrieks and he heads out. At the door he hesitates.

I am not a man of action, the practical side of things – medicine – cabinetry – route planning and so on were never my – the life of the mind, you understand? – that was my –

The whistle shrieks again and he bundles her onto the cart and rushes away with her as the whistle shrieks again and the train careers into the night.

End of the First Dream.

Second Dream

*The sound of the train takes us to an ice bound railway waiting
room converted to army field headquarters. Telegraph and phone
wires are strung everywhere and phones ring non-stop in
curiously delicate tones, answered by harassed STAFF
OFFICERS.*

*In charge of everything is the fearsome White General ROMAN
KHLUDOV, dictating to his aide, the long suffering CAPTAIN
GOLOVAN, who is pounding away at a typewriter.*

KHLUDOV. 'You ask to what we can attribute, comma, my dear
Arch Duke, comma, the succession of defeats we have suffered
over the past months full stop. Could it be that our adversaries
have not felt inclined to behave as if we were on manoeuvre in
front of the Tsar and obediently roll over and die, question
mark. Perhaps some of our foremost military men believe the
war is an extension of chess or the ballet, full stop. This,
comma, unfortunately, comma, does not appear to be the view
of the Red Guards and their commanders and until they
sportingly decide to make their own blunders I cannot see any
hope for improvement in our tactical or strategic circumstances
full stop.' Signed Khludov etc.'

*As he signs the letter the STAFF OFFICERS take phone
messages, turn to him for orders.*

FIRST STAFF OFFICER. Third battalion – heavy losses –
permission to withdraw?

SECOND STAFF OFFICER. Artillery – down to last few rounds –
continue engagement?

THIRD STAFF OFFICER. Wounded and dying – no doctors or
nurses – leave them behind?

Calmly dealing with each in turn –

KHLUDOV. Yes – no – yes –

FOURTH STAFF OFFICER. What's to be done with the deserters
we captured, sir?

FIFTH STAFF OFFICER. The baggage train – what's to be done
with it?

SIXTH STAFF OFFICER. The Red prisoners, sir – what do we do with them?

KHLUDOV. Shoot them – burn it – shoot them.

A COSSACK *marches the cowed and terrified civilian* STATIONMASTER *into the room.*

COSSACK. The Stationmaster, sir.

KHLUDOV. Strange things are happening, Stationmaster. An armoured train has been suddenly struck with paralysis. It has been steaming at full speed towards us without moving. It is hurtling down the track at eighty miles an hour for hours and yet it's still stuck exactly where it was when it started.

STATIONMASTER. The Taganash line is blocked by snow and ice, General. The points are frozen stiff.

KHLUDOV (*sniffs and points at nearby stove*). Is that stove safe, Captain Golovan? Be a fine thing for Field Headquarters to be wiped out because of fumes from a waiting room stove.

(*To* STATIONMASTER.) Snow and ice in November? How. unusual.

STATIONMASTER. With all respect, General, it is unusual at this time of year in the Crimea.

KHLUDOV (*sniffing again*). You know, I really can smell fumes from that stove.

CAPTAIN GOLOVAN. Fumes, sir? Sure, sir?

KHLUDOV (*Turning back to the* STATIONMASTER). I don't know why but I get this feeling you're on very good terms with the Bolsheviks, Stationmaster.

STATIONMASTER. Me sir? No sir.

KHLUDOV. If that's the case you can speak frankly, we shouldn't hide our convictions even in the middle of a civil war, the exchange of sincerely held views, faults on both sides etc etc.

STATIONMASTER. I'm a loyal Russian, sir. I didn't sleep for days when they shot the Tsar.

KHLUDOV. Nobody loves us, Golovan. That's our tragedy, that's the root of all our problems. (*Looking closely at the* STATIONMASTER.) Wouldn't you say there's a kind of cunning look to him? – although maybe it's a trick of the light. And when you think about those poisonous fumes and this armoured train that mysteriously can't get through – What do you make of it?

CAPTAIN GOLOVAN. Doesn't look good, sir. Not at all. Irregular. Suspicious.

KHLUDOV. It doesn't look good, does it?

STATIONMASTER (*finding his voice with desperation*). There's six foot of snow out there. I lost the tips of my fingers trying to move the points by hand. I haven't slept or eaten in thirty hours. I haven't seen my wife or children in days.

A sad look at GOLOVAN.

KHLUDOV. You can't do anything without love, even fight a war. If the train isn't on the main line with the signal at green in fifteen minutes you will shoot one man in ten of the work crew and hang the Stationmaster from the signal gantry for sabotage.

CAPTAIN GOLOVAN. One man in ten, hang the Stationmaster, yes sir.

With a strangled cry the STATIONMASTER *grabs a phone behind a partition and belabours his own deputy.*

STATIONMASTER. Now look, get that train here in ten minutes or I swear to God I'll have you shot for sabotage, I'll denounce you myself, you bastard, just get the bloody thing here, you hear me, get that bloody train here –

There's the distant sound of a brass band playing a waltz as the STATIONMASTER *slams the phone down, quivering with rage and fear.*

KHLUDOV. What's that? A waltz?

CAPTAIN GOLOVAN. General Charnota, sir. Fighting retreat. Due any moment.

Heading back to KHLUDOV.

STATIONMASTER. Beg leave to report, sir, I've given the orders.

KHLUDOV. Make sure they're carried out this time.

Beat.

Any children?

STATIONMASTER. Six, sir. Olga's the youngest but all of them are babies, really, none of them even go to school yet.

KHLUDOV. Time's getting on, isn't it? Any sign of that train?

STATIONMASTER. I guarantee it'll be here in fifteen minutes, General.

The band gives a final flourish, the door opens and
CHARNOTA *heads in with* KRAPILIN *and* LYUSKA. *The*
frantic STATIONMASTER *passes them on the way out.*

CHARNOTA. I'm here. We made it. Most of us. Some of us.
A few of us.

Looking distastefully out through the open door –

What exactly is going on here, Roman?

KHLUDOV. Why don't you mind your own business?

CHARNOTA (*shrugs*). So what now?

He snaps his heels, salutes.

General Charnota reporting for orders, sir.

KHLUDOV. Your orders, my dear Grisha are - your orders are - to
take your men to the Karpov Gorge and there you will – you
will hold the line, that's what you'll do, yes, you'll hold the
line.

CHARNOTA. What line?

KHLUDOV. The line. You asked for orders and I'm giving them
to you.

CHARNOTA. Hold the line?

KHLUDOV. That's what I want you to do.

CHARNOTA. At Karpov Gorge?

A sigh from CHARNOTA *as he turns back to* LYUSKA.

CHARNOTA. Karpov Gorge. Totally indefensible.

LYUSKA. You can't go.

CHARNOTA (*shrugs*). I asked for orders, he gave them to me.

LYUSKA. It'll be a total disaster.

CHARNOTA. Of course it'll be a disaster.

LYUSKA. I'm coming with you.

CHARNOTA. You should stay and look after the wounded.

LYUSKA. I promised I'd stay with you, whatever happens,
wherever the war takes you.

She gives him a fierce and passionate kiss.

If he's sending you to die at Karpov Gorge, I'll die with you.

KRAPILIN. Me, too, sir? I'm to come and die, too?

CHARNOTA. You stay here, Krapilin. De Brisard was right, you're the worst soldier in the army and that's saying something.

The band strikes up as he grabs LYUSKA *by the hand and heads out, passing the* STATIONMASTER *rushing back in, holding his young daughter,* OLGA *by the hand.*

STATIONMASTER. Wishing to report sir –

KHLUDOV. You've done it? The armoured train? On the main line? Signal at green?

STATIONMASTER. Green, General, green green green.

He collapses on his knees and GOLOVAN *stares at* OLGA.

CAPTAIN GOLOVAN. Child – ? military headquarters – ? what is that child doing here? Irregular, highly irregular. Unheard of.

STATIONMASTER. She's Olga my youngest, I thought the General might like to see her.

He fumbles something out of his pocket.

STATIONMASTER. My medal, General, for twenty years service.

KHLUDOV (*looking up*). Who's that?

CAPTAIN GOLOVAN. Daughter of the Stationmaster, sir. Won't happen again.

KHLUDOV. Olga, isn't it? Come here, Olga –

As she dutifully stands in front of him PARAMON KORZUKHIN *enters, whispers urgently to* GOLOVAN.

KHLUDOV. I want you to promise me, Olga, that you'll never start smoking. My doctors tell me it's killing me, it's bad for my nerves and they give me sweets instead but they don't help, so I always have a pocketful of sweets. Would you like a sweet, Olga?

She nods and he indicates his trouser's pocket.

If you want one you have to reach in and take it.

STATIONMASTER (*choking*). Take it, darling – take the sweet, my dear.

In dead silence she feels inside KHLUDOV *'s trouser pocket, pulls out a sweet and puts it into her mouth. The Brass Band plays* CHARNOTA *'s waltz outside again, then stops abruptly.*

KHLUDOV. Now run along and remember – no cigars.

On shaky legs the STATIONMASTER *shepherds* OLGA *out as* GOLOVAN *pockets the money* KORZUKHIN *palms him and announces his presence.*

CAPTAIN GOLOVAN. Deputy Minister for Trade – on official business. Travelling for days. Confidential interview, most grateful.

KORZUKHIN. Paramon Korzukhin – and may I say how honoured I am to finally meet the man on whom the future of Russian depends –

KHLUDOV (*ignoring the proffered handshake*). I'm listening, Korzukhin – but you really had better be the Deputy Minister for Trade.

KORZUKHIN. The Council of Ministers has instructed me to determine the whereabouts of the five workmen who were illegally arrested at Simferol and brought here on your orders.

KHLUDOV. You didn't see them on your way in?

KORZUKHIN. No –

KHLUDOV. Captain Golovan, be so good as to show the Deputy Minister the prisoners.

GOLOVAN *takes* KORZUKHIN *to the door, points into the air. A shudder from* KORZUKHIN *as he keeps staring upwards.*

KORZUKHIN. You hung them all?

KHLUDOV. Count them for me, Golovan.

CAPTAIN GOLOVAN. Two three four five – they're all there, sir.

KHLUDOV. Was there anything else, Korzukhin? We're trying to fight a war here, you know.

GOLOVAN *slams the door shut and a badly rattled* KORZUKHIN *tries to rally.*

KORZUKHIN. There is also a matter which involves my own Ministry. A strategically important shipment has been held up here for weeks. It's vitally important to the war effort that it gets through.

KHLUDOV. What is it? Guns? Uniforms?

KORZUKHIN. Fur coats.

KHLUDOV. Fur coats?

KORZUKHIN. Fur coats for export. I have the waybill here.

KHLUDOV. May I see it?

He takes it, examines it.

Signed by, countersigned by – yes, everything appears to be in order –

Handing it to GOLOVAN.

Captain Golovan – shunt all the wagons shown on this waybill onto a siding, pour petrol on them and set fire to them.

CAPTAIN GOLOVAN. Waybill, siding, petrol, yes sir.

KORZUKHIN. You can't do that.

KHLUDOV. If the Deputy Minister tries to stop you, shoot him.

CAPTAIN GOLOVAN. Shoot him, sir, yes sir.

As GOLOVAN *leaves,* KORZUKHIN *swallows hard, tries to rally once again.*

KORZUKHIN. The Council of Ministers – the Council of Ministers has authorized me to bring back a report on the military position in the Crimea.

KHLUDOV. The position? The position?

Rage overmasters him as he shakes his fist in KORZUKHIN's *face.*

I'll tell you what the position is. The position is that we have no food, medical supplies or ammunition. I asked for men and I was sent a birthday present of Kuban Cossacks without, however, any boots for them they can't do anything but sit around like so many parrots on stools –

He controls himself with a deep breath and a death's head smile.

In consequence we're bored, very bored, I think you can tell the Council of Ministers that, yes, that would sum it up, that's the position.

KORZUKHIN. What should I tell them about our chances?

KHLUDOV. Tell them to start packing their bags and make a run for it, like you appear to be doing.

KORZUKHIN. You've gone too far, Khludov. I shall report your remarks and your attitude to the Commander In Chief.

KHLUDOV. Please do so. You may also tell your fellow crooks that their whores in Paris are going to have to do without their fur coats this winter.

The sound of a train arriving and the STATIONMASTER *rushes in again, followed by the* COMMANDER IN CHIEF *and* ATHANASIUS.

STATIONMASTER. Special just in from Kerman Kemalchi, sir.

KHLUDOV. Here's the Commander in Chief, Korzukhin. You can speak to him personally.

COMMANDER IN CHIEF. Is it true, Khludov? Have the Reds taken Tushun?

KHLUDOV. It is my sad duty to report that they did so three hours ago. The Bolsheviks are in the Crimea, yes.

COMMANDER IN CHIEF. Are we finished?

KHLUDOV. Finished, yes, I rather think so.

COMMANDER IN CHIEF. Then there's only one thing to do. Archbishop –

ATHANASIUS (*falling to his knees*). Abandoned by the Western powers, stabbed in the back by the treacherous Poles, Holy Mother Russia cries aloud for succour, Lord, in her hour of tribulation –

KHLUDOV. Excuse me, Your Grace, but is it really worth bothering the Almighty with this? He may not, after all, be on our side and if he is, he's not done much of a job up to now for us, has he?

ATHANASIUS. This is blasphemy –

COMMANDER IN CHIEF. Worse, it's defeatism. My God, Khludov, listen to yourself. I should have made you take that rest cure this summer. A spa, mineral water, light massage – it would have made a new man of you.

KHLUDOV. And meantime who would have been fighting across Russia yard by yard? Who would have ordered Charnota and the others to make a totally unnecessary and doomed last stand at Karpov Gorge? Who, may I ask, would have been your hangman?

COMMANDER IN CHIEF. That's quite enough –

He fumbles a letter from his tunic.

This is a personal letter from me to the officers and men. You'll be so good as to read it to them.

KHLUDOV. So you knew this was going to happen? You saw it coming?

COMMANDER IN CHIEF. I won't warn you again –

The door flies open and DE BRISARD *crashes through, his head bandaged, leaning on* GOLOVAN *for support.* KORZUKHIN *looks at the orange glow in the background, in anguish.*

KORZUKHIN. My furs –

DE BRISARD (*to* KHLUDOV). Good evening, your Imperial Majesty –

(*Sings.*) Countess, for one rendezvous with you I'll tell you the secrets of my heart –

CAPTAIN GOLOVAN. Colonel Count De Brisard, sir, Commander of the Hussars. Head wounds and concussion.

COMMANDER IN CHIEF. Put him on my train to Sebastopol.

KHLUDOV. Sebastopol, sir?

COMMANDER IN CHIEF. I'm leaving you in charge. The headquarters will be moved to Sebastopol, too.

KHLUDOV. Sebastopol?

COMMANDER IN CHIEF. The Crimea, must I spell it out, has been lost. It's all rather gone smash, I'm afraid. Make sure you read them the letter.

As he heads for the door, KORZUKHIN *steps forward.*

KORZUKHIN. Paramon Korzukhin, Deputy Minister for Trade. Allow me to accompany you –

KHLUDOV. You're staying here, Korzukhin, until we get to the bottom of who exactly you are and what you're up to. (*To* KRAPILIN.) Shoot him if he moves.

The despairing KORZUKHIN *watches helplessly as the* COMMANDER IN CHIEF *and* ATHANASIUS *leave. As they reach the door.*

KHLUDOV. And Charnota and the others? What are they to do? Fight to the last man? Lay down their lives so you can make it to the boats?

COMMANDER IN CHIEF. One more word – just one more –

Shamefaced, he leaves with DE BRISARD *and* ATHANASIUS *as* KHLUDOV *watches them go with contempt. He opens the letters as the* STAFF OFFICERS *cluster around, scans it with a yawn.*

KHLUDOV. Soldiers – the Russians people – temporary withdrawal – General Kutyepov, disengage, Sebastopol, embark – Kalinin and Don Cossacks, entrain, Sebastopol – Headquarters, reestablished, Sebastopol –

(*Coolly folding the letter up.*) Nothing very new there.

FIRST STAFF OFFICER. Our orders, sir?

SECOND STAFF OFFICER. What about us?

THIRD STAFF OFFICER. What do we do?

KHLUDOV. Really, gentlemen – I should have thought that was obvious.

GOLOVAN *and the other officers start to pull the maps down, tear up files, push papers into the remaining stoves which billow white smoke. Through the smoke appears the figure of* GOLUBKOV, *supporting* SERAFIMA, *who appears to be in the last stages of fever.*

SERAFIMA. Khludov – Roman Khludov – which of you is Roman Khludov?

CAPTAIN GOLOVAN. Someone else to see you, General.

SERAFIMA *lets go of* GOLUBKOV, *loses her balance, gets it back, draws herself up to her full height.*

SERAFIMA. Since I left St. Petersburg all I heard was Khludov, Khludov, Khludov – Khludov knows what he's doing, Khludov is the Saviour of Mother Russia – What I didn't know was that to find General Khludov I would have to pass rows of hanged men with sacks over their heads and the bodies of women and children –

The alarmed GOLUBKOV *tries to intervene.*

GOLUBKOV. Pay no attention to her. She's delirious, she doesn't know what she's saying.

KHLUDOV. Good. In my experience when people do know what they're saying you can't believe a word of it.

GOLUBKOV. She has typhus.

KHLUDOV. I have a cure for typhus. It even works on communists.

GOLUBKOV. She's not a communist. She's trying to find her husband, Korzukhin, the Deputy Minister for Trade.

KHLUDOV *barks a savage laugh.*

KHLUDOV. So you're not just a crook, Korzukhin – you're married to a Communist, are you?

GOLUBKOV. Korzukhin? It's really you?

SERAFIMA. Thank God you made it out of St. Petersburg, too.

KORZUKHIN. You're speaking to me?

SERAFIMA. Paramon –

KORZUKHIN (*avoiding her desperate embrace*). St. Petersburg? No, I'm not expecting anyone from St. Petersburg and I've never seen this woman or this man in my life.

GOLUBKOV. Well no, you don't know me of course, but your own wife –

KORZUKHIN. This must be some kind of blackmail, yes, that's what it is –

GOLUBKOV. She's travelled thousands of miles to see you. She's been starved, frozen stiff, but through it all she's never given up.

SERAFIMA. Paramon, please – remember our little house, the honeymoon – surely you remember that?

KORZUKHIN. Sorry, not a thing.

Her strength goes and she topples into GOLUBKOV's *arms.*

GOLUBKOV (*to* KHLUDOV). He's exactly how she described him. Can't you do something?

KHLUDOV. I'm a soldier, not a matchmaker. And what exactly is your interest in another man's wife?

GOLUBKOV. She needed help. There was no one else.

KHLUDOV. Captain Golovan, open a file on these three and put them all on the train under guard. We'll continue this investigation in Sebastopol.

KRAPILIN steps forward, clears his throat.

KRAPILIN. Permission to speak, sir – Trifomin Krapilin, sir, I was one of the men you sent to be slaughtered at Perekop. We all expected to die there but you didn't kill quite as many of us as you usually did. Although you made up for it in the next couple of battles when you finished almost everybody off –

KHLUDOV. Get to the point, Krapilin.

KRAPILIN. The thing is, sir, ever since then I can't shake the feeling that somehow you overlooked me, that I'm some kind of mistake.

KHLUDOV. Mistake?

KRAPILIN. I'm not the kind of man who pushes himself forward, I never have been, which is maybe why I've stayed a private or maybe I'm just not cut out for the military – anyway, I've been thinking you might have lost sight of me, being so busy and all, retreating, hanging people, retreating again – Trimofin Krapilin. I was at Perekop, you see –

KHLUDOV. Excuse me one moment, Krapilin – (*To* GOLOVAN.) I think I'm going to need a board, about this big, and some string – (*To* KRAPILIN.) I'm so sorry. Carry on.

KRAPILIN. I didn't want you overlooking me again, so if you're wondering where I got to, I wanted to step forward.

KHLUDOV. I've done my share of fighting, Krapilin. I was wounded twice at Chonggar.

KRAPILIN. At Chonggar, you bloody madman, if you'll excuse me calling you that, sir, you ordered the Regimental Band to march ahead of us, playing at the top of their lungs. Why did you do that? What was the point of it? Was there any point? And all these people you've been arresting and hanging? Did you have to hang them?

KHLUDOV. You've been thinking a lot about this, I can tell.

KRAPILIN. It's shoot him and hang her and set fire to this and all the time we just keep going backwards.

KHLUDOV. There's a lot of sense in what you say about how to make war, Krapilin but I don't think I have the time at the moment to deal with the points you raise one by one – (*To* GOLOVAN.) The board?

CAPTAIN GOLOVAN. Here, sir. Board, sir.

KHLUDOV. Be so good as to take this man outside, make sure of the spelling of his name and hang him from any available lamp post as a Bolshevik. Is that what you wanted, Krapilin? Are you happy now?

KRAPILIN. To be hung, sir? Happy to be hung, no, sir, I'm not. I'm not at all happy.

KHLUDOV. What's done is done, Krapilin. I'm sure you wouldn't want me to go back on my decision.

KRAPILIN. No sir but on the other hand I didn't know what I was saying, I don't know what came over me –

He falls to his knees.

KRAPILIN. I don't want to be hung, sir, I really don't –

KHLUDOV. Come on, Krapilin – you got it off your chest, made an honest man of yourself by saying what's on your mind and now you have to hang for it. I can't see what you've got to complain about, can you?

KRAPILIN. When you put it like that, sir – no.

KHLUDOV. You began well, Krapilin, but to finish on your knees – it's not good enough.

Captain GOLOVAN *hauls* KRAPILIN *to his feet.*

When you've hung him, lock these three Communists on the train.

As GOLOVAN *marches* GOLUBKOV, SERAFIMA *and* KORZUKHIN *off,* GOLUBKOV *is moved to apologise to her.*

GOLUBKOV. I'm sorry. I seem to have made a mess of it.

KORZUKHIN. You have, haven't you?

The STAFF OFFICERS *scramble to the doors, leaving* KHLUDOV *alone. He reaches for a phone.*

KHLUDOV. Khludov here. Tell the commander of the armoured train to head for Taganash firing at everything he sees. When he gets there he's to level the town, I don't want one brick on top of another. When that's done he's to head for Sebastopol ripping up the track behind him. That'll give them something to remember Roman Khludov by.

A huge explosion blows the waiting room wall down – outside can be seen a row of hanged men, with KRAPILIN *kicking his legs in his death agonies. A board with* PRIVATE KRAPILIN – BOLSHEVIK *is hung around his neck. Fingers still on his pulse,* KHLUDOV *hardly seems to notice the devastation.*

I think I must be going down with something.

The terrified OLGA *runs in, disoriented by the massive blast.*

Olga – another sweet?

As she steps forward the STATIONMASTER *rushes in, panicking.*

STATIONMASTER. Olga – Olga – where are you? Olga darling –

KHLUDOV. Here – in my pocket – you remember?

As she reaches for his pocket the STATIONMASTER *pulls her away from* KHLUDOV *and gathers her in his arms.*

STATIONMASTER. The train's about to leave for Sebastopol. Shouldn't you be on it?

KHLUDOV *shrugs, puts his hand in his pocket and gives her the sweets.*

KHLUDOV. Have them all, my dear. Help yourself.

STATIONMASTER. Hold daddy's hand and don't let go this time.

A contemptuous look at KHLUDOV *and he heads to the door with her.*

STATIONMASTER. This way darling, this way – don't look over there –

Picking her up, he hurries out, shielding her from the dead men. KHLUDOV *stares thoughtfully at* KRAPILIN.

KHLUDOV. Yes, I really think I'm going down with something . . .

Another blast levels any wall that remains and the ceiling falls in all around KHLUDOV *as the train whistles again as it speeds into the night.*

End of Second Dream.

Third Dream

Ships' hooters sound as the lights rise on the interior of the offices of the White Counter Intelligence in a commandeered building on the dock side Sebastopol. A long line of REFUGEES, *desperate to leave, pushes and shoves for the attention of the* GUARDS, *who are busy taking bribes and looting the luggage.*

To one side is an empty cubicle, into which GOLUBKOV *is escorted by* GUARDS. *One entire wall is covered in files and more boxes of files spill their contents on the floor. The* GUARDS *leave and* TIKHI *enters, closes the door carefully behind him. In the centre of his office is a large box containing a table and chair. Wires wreathe around it, giving it a sinister appearance.* TIKHI *surveys* GOLUBKOV *for a long moment, then asks him something in a conversational tone –*

TIKHI. Do you?

GOLUBKOV. Do I what?

TIKHI. You know, do you?

GOLUBKOV. I'm sorry – ?

> TIKHI*'s hand goes into his pocket and he brings out a packet of cigarettes.*

TIKHI. Do you smoke?

GOLUBKOV. I'm not sure.

> *He thinks about it.*

> No, no I don't.

> *A long silence.*

TIKHI. Are you afraid of me, pal?

GOLUBKOV. That's a very difficult question to answer.

> *Another silence and then* GOLUBKOV *gathers up his nerve to ask.*

> How is she?

TIKHI. Who?

GOLUBKOV. Serafima Korzukhin. This is all a terrible misunderstanding –

TIKHI *reaches towards him and slams his fist on the desk beside him. He shows him the bug he's crushed.*

TIKHI. A cockroach. You know what's worse than a cockroach? A Bolshevik. A Bolshevik who spreads rumours about what happens in here, what we do to you when we get hold of you, because if we did half the things they say we do we'd be monsters, and do I look like a monster to you or do I look like an ordinary man?

What do you think I did before the Revolution?

GOLUBKOV (*nervous*). It's very hard to tell what people are just by looking at them.

TIKHI. I was a plumber. (*Sadly.*) You say you were a student, right, and I'd say you never gave a moment's thought to plumbing, you have that kind of intellectual look about you. But it was there all the time, behind the wall, under your feet, pipes going into the house, pipes going out, thousands of miles of them. (*Injured.*) You've no right to be afraid of me. You got to Sebastopol in one piece, didn't you – you and your lady friend.

GOLUBKOV. Serafima Korzukhin is a total stranger to me.

TIKHI. You were arrested at the same time.

GOLUBKOV. Half of the Ukraine was arrested.

TIKHI. She used abusive language to the Chief of Staff.

GOLUBKOV. She was delirious, she had typhus. Is she still ill? Is she alive?

TIKHI (*morosely ignoring the questions*). Pants down, do your business, pants up, pull the chain, not a thought, until one day something goes wrong and then you're screaming blue murder for a plumber and it's Yes Sir, No Sir, Three Bloody Bags Full Sir and then you forget all about us until the next time, how do you think we feel? (*Reaching for a file.*) The first thing I need to know is your real name.

A groan from GOLUBKOV.

GOLUBKOV. I've told you – how many times do I have to tell you – my name is Sergei Pavlovich Golubkov, I was a student in St. Petersburg, I was trying to return my library books –

TIKHI (*interrupting*). You seem to think this whole business is a bunch of laughs. The Reds took fifty hostages, young boys, Army Cadets, at Taganrog and threw them one at a time into a blast furnace. Was that something to laugh about?

GOLUBKOV. That's nothing to do with me.

TIKHI. I want you to step in there, my old mate.

He opens the door to the box, ushers the nervous GOLUBKOV *inside and closes the door. He turns a lever and sparks shoot from the wires, as they glow with a threatening hum.*

From now on when you lie to me I shall turn this handle, you understand? Now, once again – name?

GOLUBKOV's *voice sounds tinnily on the speakers.*

GOLUBKOV. Sergei . . . Pavlovich . . . Golubkov.

TIKHI. Place of residence?

GOLUBKOV. St. Petersburg.

TIKHI. Your reasons for leaving Soviet Russia and smuggling yourself into White territory with a known Communist agent impersonating the wife of an important Minister?

GOLUBKOV. I believe that Serafima Korzukhin really is who she says she is and all I did was try to help her when she was sick.

TIKHI (*reaching for another file*). 'When brought face to face with the woman the man denied all knowledge of her – ' That's what you told me, right?

GOLUBKOV. I think so, more or less, yes –

TIKHI. Can't have it both ways, can you?

GOLUBKOV. What if he was lying? What if he had something to hide? What if he was just – I don't know – bored with her and this was a chance to get rid of her?

TIKHI. You're trying to tell me the entire revolution was just a trick of Korzukhin to dump his wife?

GOLUBKOV. No, of course not – but surely you can make him tell the truth. Put him in there.

TIKHI. Paramon Korzukhin is no longer a subject of our enquiries.

GOLUBKOV. You let him go?

TIKHI. Captain Golovan and him took off. Just like everybody else with any sense is doing.

GOLUBKOV. Then why are we still here?

TIKHI. Because you're still under investigation.

GOLUBKOV. But what does it matter if everybody's leaving, if the war's lost?

TIKHI. Now what kind of attitude is that? I'm surprised at you.

The machine gives an ominous hum.

Now read me your statement.

GOLUBKOV. I haven't made a statement.

TIKHI. I'll dictate it.

The machine gives another ominous hum and GOLUBKOV *groans in fear, sits at the desk, picks up the pencil that's on it waiting by the sheet of paper.*

TIKHI. Why don't you sign it first in case you forget?

GOLUBKOV. Tell me what I want to say –

He starts to write to TIKHI*'s dictation.*

TIKHI. 'I, the undersigned on this day the thirty first of October 1920 at the Counter Intelligence Section of the Southern Front Headquarters declare that the wife of Paramon Korzukhin, Serafima Vladimirovna Korzukhin – '

A hesitation from GOLUBKOV.

What's the matter?

GOLUBKOV. Just writing her name – (*A lovesick sigh.*) I'm sorry – carry on –

He controls himself and keeps on writing.

TIKHI. 'Serafima Vladimitrovna Korzukhin, to my personal knowledge a member of the Communist party – '

GOLUBKOV. I don't know she's any such thing.

TIKHI. But you don't know she's not.

GOLUBKOV. That's true, but –

TIKHI. Let's give her the benefit of the doubt, shall we?

The bemused GOLUBKOV *recommences writing as the machine hums ominously again.*

'Entered the territory occupied by the armed forces of Southern Russia for the purposes of spreading Bolshevik propaganda and establishing contact with the Communist underground in the town of Sebastopol – '

GOLUBKOV. She'd no intention of coming to Sebastopol. That madman Khludov had her kidnapped and brought here. She nearly died on the train.

Ignoring it, TIKHI *opens the door and takes the sheet from him.*

TIKHI. I never had a shred of doubt you'd come to your senses and co-operate. You're a free man again. Congratulations. Case dismissed without a stain on your underpants.

GOLUBKOV. I can go? And Serafima?

TIKHI. Her? She's done for, mate.

TIKHI *bangs a bell and shouts.*

Send Skunsky in – (*To* GOLUBKOV.) You can go if you like.

GOLUBKOV. Done for?

TIKHI. Finito. Cashed her chips.

GOLUBKOV. I withdraw my statement.

TIKHI. Don't play silly buggers. And I wouldn't hang around Sebastopol too long if I was you.

A Guard enters and marches GOLUBKOV *off as the sinister* SKUNSKY *enters by another door.*

SKUNSKY. You're letting him go?

TIKHI. Who? I can't even remember his name. (*Pushing the 'confession' across the desk.*) Read this. Careful – the ink's still wet.

SKUNSKY *reads it.*

SKUNSKY. Whose handwriting's this?

TIKHI. Very readable, isn't it?

SKUNSKY. The Deputy Minister for Trade is married to a Bolshevik?

TIKHI. How much would that statement be worth to him, would you say? If he wanted to keep his head on his shoulders?

SKUNSKY. Here? – ten thousand dollars. A lot less once he gets to Constantinople and out of our hands.

TIKHI. Go and arrest Korzukhin again, he'll be at the docks, trying to get a ship out. Bring him back and that son of a bitch Golovan too, if you find him.

SKUNSKY. What's it worth?

TIKHI. Two thousand dollars.

SKUNSKY. Make it three.

TIKHI. Two and a half and you get to work on the missis again personally when I've finished with her.

He bangs the bell.

Send the woman in.

As SKUNSKY *heads out another door opens and an* ORDERLY *brings* SERAFIMA *in.*

I won't keep you long, love, just a few formalities, tie up a few loose ends, then you can go.

SERAFIMA. I can leave?

TIKHI. It's Liberty Hall here, of course you can, pet. All I want you to do is admit you and hubby came here to spread Communist propaganda and organize armed resistance and Bob's Your Uncle.

SERAFIMA. If I admit that you'll shoot me.

TIKHI. I'm a little deaf in this ear – a gas boiler blew up in it.

Indicating the chair and desk inside the box.

Park yourself in there and enjoy yourself.

SERAFIMA. I'm not a complete fool.

TIKHI. Take a squint at this.

He shows her GOLUBKOV's *statement, forces her to read it..*

See the name at the bottom?

SERAFIMA. Sergei Golubkov never wrote this.

TIKHI. My eyes aren't too good since I got some drain cleaner squirted into them by accident but it looks like a G and an O and an L –

SERAFIMA. Golubkov? No –

TIKHI. That's it, Golubkov.

SERAFIMA. What did you do to him to make him write this about me?

TIKHI. You know what they're like, these high strung, intellectual types – Now where were we? Look, I'll write CONFESSION at the top of the page, get you started –

He takes a sheer of paper and starts to write.

'I, Serafima Vladimitrovna Korzukhin entered White territory to engage in Red propaganda and encourage rebellion – '

SERAFIMA. I never said that –

TIKHI. My other ear's playing up now. I banged the side of my head on some ducting and I think I knocked something out of place.

The box gives another threatening hum and TIKHI *opens the door and thrusts her inside.*

Lies, lies, I don't want to hear any more lies. Any time you tell me lies I shall turn this handle – or would you rather deal with Skunsky? You might have seen him on your way in – tall thin chap whose family were all murdered by the Reds, is that what you want, for Skunsky to go to work on you – ?

Offstage we hear CHARNOTA*'s Brass Band playing the waltz again. Instantly he stops, listens with a smile on his face.*

That's nice. That's very nice. That'll be General Charnota, he's known for his musical selections.

SERAFIMA*'s voice sounds as tinnily as* GOLUBKOV*'s did.*

SERAFIMA. General Charnota?

TIKHI. He'll be sodding off with the rest of them.

SERAFIMA. Would you – would you like to dance?

TIKHI. That's very irregular. That's a very strange thing to ask me.

SERAFIMA. These aren't normal times, are they?

TIKHI. You can say that again.

SERAFIMA. Well?

He tentatively enters the box and overcoming her aversion for him, she reaches for him.

Put your arm on my waist, just like that –

Bashfully TIKHI *takes her around the waist and starts to dance with her in the box.*

TIKHI. A waltz, eh? I do love a waltz.

As they pass the desk, seizing her chance, SERAFIMA *pushes him aside and jumps onto the desk. She starts to hammer on the roof of the box.*

SERAFIMA. General Charnota! (*To* TIKHI.)Keep away from me. Where's my husband?

TIKHI. Korzukhin? He's gone. Golovan's gone. They've all gone.

SERAFIMA. Paramon wouldn't leave without me –

TIKHI. Get down before you hurt yourself-

SERAFIMA. General Charnota! Help me –

TIKHI. That's Government property –

SERAFIMA. I don't believe he's gone, not my Paramon –

TIKHI. Suit yourself –

He makes a grab for her but falls back as CHARNOTA *slides down the ladder onto the roof of the box, gun in hand. The impatient* LYUSKA *calls from the top of the ladder.*

LYUSKA. The boat's waiting, Grisha – we don't have time for gestures –

CHARNOTA. You said you'd wait for me forever, go wherever I went –

LYUSKA. Of course, yes, but the last boat is about to leave.

SERAFIMA. General Charnota – take me with you, please. Or not, just as you choose. I don't care any more but this man, this horrible man –

A ship's hooter gives a loud blast and, fearing they'll be left behind, the GUARDS *desert their posts.* CHARNOTA *picks* SERAFIMA *up and heads off with her, leaving* TIKHI *in the box.*

TIKHI. Bugger off then and bugger the lot of you, the sight of you makes me want to throw up – out, out, everybody clear off, this is my bloody office –

SERAFIMA. Paramon!

The box hums violently and sparks shoot from it.

TIKHI. There'll be hell to pay about this, sheer bloody hell – make no mistake about that –

The ship's hooters sound again and the box starts to fill with smoke as the REFUGEES *run for the boats.*

End of the Third Dream.

Fourth Dream

The Governor's Palace in Sebastopol – a torn curtain across the window, a cracked gilt framed mirror, a white square where a picture once hung. The most striking feature is a dozen doors which line the walls of the room.

DE BRISARD *is sitting in front of the fireplace, looks up as the* COMMANDER IN CHIEF *enters briskly.*

COMMANDER IN CHIEF. How's the head, De Brisard?

DE BRISARD. Much better sir – aspirin.

Looking at his reflection in the mirror.

COMMANDER IN CHIEF. Look at me closely, Colonel. Do you see any resemblance to Alexander the Great?

DE BRISARD. Perhaps if you could show me a recent photograph – ?

COMMANDER IN CHIEF. Don't be a bloody fool.

Without warning DE BRISARD *breaks into song again.*

DE BRISARD. For just one hour with you, Countess –

COMMANDER IN CHIEF. My dear fellow, I don't think aspirin is going to do it for you. No man has done more for his country but I'm not sure I want you hanging around here feeling sorry for yourself for ever.

Time to go, Colonel, time to go.

DE BRISARD. Where? Go where, sir?

COMMANDER IN CHIEF. Leave it to me, I'll get you on some ship or other.

DE BRISARD. And afterwards?

COMMANDER IN CHIEF. I'll see that you're taken care of.

DE BRISARD. Yes sir, I appreciate that, sir. And I shall be the first to congratulate your Imperial Majesty when we finally beat the Bolsheviks and you're back in the Kremlin.

COMMANDER IN CHIEF. A word of advice, Colonel – try to control yourself a little better. It's been a strain on all of us, I know, but. the great thing is – the great thing is –

Shrugs, unable to think of it.

Why don't you run along?

DE BRISARD. Yes, Your Majesty, I'll do that.

Humming the tune he sang earlier he heads out as the
COMMANDER IN CHIEF *calls to an invisible* ORDERLY
offstage.

COMMANDER IN CHIEF. Make sure that poor old De Brisard
has an escort to a ship. And a cabin. And a note to the ship's
doctor that he needs a damn sight more than aspirin.

Wheel the others in. I'll give them three minutes apiece, it's the
least I can do.

Looking at his reflection again.

Alexander the Great?

Unseen, KORZUKHIN *and* GOLOVAN *enter.*

Nothing like him, nothing like him at all.

At a discreet cough from KORZUKHIN *he turns.*

What do you want?

KORZUKHIN. Korzukhin, Deputy Minister for Trade. The
Council of Ministers has instructed me to apply for compen-
sation for a train load of furs for export that were destroyed
by the Commander of the Crimean front –

COMMANDER IN CHIEF. Korzukhin? I was just about to send
for you. I'm so glad you dropped by. Look at me closely,
Minister, take your time and tell me – do I look like Alexander
the Great?

KORZUKHIN. Alexander the – ?

Thrusting a newspaper under his nose.

COMMANDER IN CHIEF. This newspaper says I do and you're
the publisher, aren't you? It says here, look – 'Publisher,
Paramon Korzukhin' – and a publisher, I imagine, is respon-
sible for everything. in his paper.

Pointing out the offending passage.

"The Commander in Chief, like Alexander the Great, walks up
and down the platform – "

What is that nonsense supposed to mean? Do you really think
there were railway platforms in Alexander the Great's day?
And even if there were, how in God's name could you possibly

know what he looked like, much less that I look exactly like
him? (*Getting angrier.*) It gets even worse – "One look at his
cheerful, manly face and every worm of doubt as to our
eventual victory is bound to melt away – "

KHLUDOV. Sir –

COMMANDER IN CHIEF. Good Christ, I'm a soldier and I
could write better than that. Since when have worms melted?
What in God's name is manly when applied to a man? And if
you think I'm cheerful, all I can say is Thank God you're not
around when I'm angry.

KHLUDOV. General –

COMMANDER IN CHIEF. I am hours away from being driven
ignominiously from Russian soil, perhaps for ever, with the
tattered remnants of an army that couldn't be made to fight and
I'm forced to read this arse-licking drivel with its incoherent
flights of sycophantic fantasy and incompetent punctuation.

Rest assured, when we get to Constantinople. I'll have you
court martialled for your prose style alone.

Am I shouting? Does your head hurt? Try aspirin.

*He strides out through one of the doors, slamming the door
and* KORZUKHIN *turns to* GOLOVAN.

KORZUKHIN. Well I can't say I didn't bring it on myself – to
complain to one lunatic about another and he seems an even
bigger lunatic than Khludov.

CAPTAIN GOLOVAN. What do we do now?

KORZUKHIN. What do you say to Paris, Captain Golovan? The
Seine, the cafés, the boulevards?

CAPTAIN GOLOVAN. It sounds better than being hung for
desertion.

KORZUKHIN *snaps his fingers,* GOLOVAN *picks up his bags
and they exit as* KHLUDOV *enters by another door. At the
same time* ATHANASIUS *enters by a third.*

KHLUDOV. Archbishop Athanasius. Did you send that Bible to
Headquarters for me?

ATHANASIUS. In the circumstances I thought –

KHLUDOV. I read it on the train here. Then I got bored and threw
it out of the window. The only lines I remember are – 'The
enemy said I will pursue, I will overtake, I will divide the
spoils, my lust shall be satisfied on them'.

Now would you say a madman could remember those lines?

ATHANASIUS (*cautious*). I think it would be very difficult for him.

KHLUDOV. I even remember they're from Exodus.

ATHANASIUS. That's something a madman certainly wouldn't remember.

KHLUDOV (*relieved*). No more Bibles, Archbishop – they're blasphemous and defeatist. Why are you hanging around here anyway?

ATHANASIUS. I am waiting to see the Commander In Chief.

KHLUDOV. You know what you'll get if you wait too long – the Reds.

ATHANASIUS. How near are they?

KHLUDOV. I admire your spirit, I really do. Here are you and I calmly swapping quotations from the Bible and at this very moment the Red cavalry is heading to Sebastopol to crucify every priest it catches. They nail them to doors, you know. That's the good thing about a civil war, it brings out the best in people.

Sobbing with terror again, ATHANASIUS *heads to the doors, chooses one at random, dives through as the* COMMANDER IN CHIEF *steps in through another. There's a distinct coolness between the two men, masked by a frigid politeness.*

COMMANDER IN CHIEF. Everybody safely on board, Khludov?

KHLUDOV. Pretty much so, sir.

COMMANDER IN CHIEF. Life preservers and ships' biscuits and so on? Bit of a mystery all this to me, I don't mind admitting, this naval business.

KHLUDOV. Taken care of sir. I imagine. The Imperial Navy, what's left of it and all that.

COMMANDER IN CHIEF. You got here safely then?

KHLUDOV. It appears so.

COMMANDER IN CHIEF. Journey all right?

KHLUDOV. I made them get me a corner seat so nobody would keep tripping over my feet all night. Pulled the blind down, read, slept, a little light refreshment here and there, help the hours go by – you know the kind of thing.

COMMANDER IN CHIEF. Nothing out of the ordinary then?

KHLUDOV. Now you mention it, as a matter of fact there was.

At one point the light went out and I thought about something that happened when I was a boy. I went into the kitchen when it was dark. There were cockroaches all over the floor, the stove, along the shelves, probably hanging upside down from the ceiling too.

Lit a match, they started to run. Match went out – all I heard was their tiny little feet – tip tip tip tip tip, off they went. Just like in the retreat, your masterfully organized retreat, sir.

COMMANDER IN CHIEF (*controlling his temper*). I have you to thank, General, for your great strategic and battle fighting skills that were such a vital contribution to what you are good enough to call my retreat.

KHLUDOV. I wouldn't wish to take an ounce of credit away from you.

COMMANDER IN CHIEF. I saw those men you hanged. And the women and the children, too. I never ordered that.

KHLUDOV. No, you just told me what was expected of me and left me to get on with it. If we'd won, guess who'd have got the medals?

COMMANDER IN CHIEF (*abruptly turning away*). I shan't keep you any longer. I'm moving to a hotel for the night.

KHLUDOV. Nearer to the harbour?

COMMANDER IN CHIEF. You're very close to being arrested, Khludov.

KHLUDOV. My bodyguard is in the hall. I'm very popular with them. Somehow they still have the impression that I know what I'm doing. Remarkable, when you think about it.

COMMANDER IN CHIEF. A rest cure wouldn't have done you any good at all, would it? You hate me.

KHLUDOV. Of course I hate you.

COMMANDER IN CHIEF. It's that that's kept you going these past few months.

KHLUDOV. You even want to take the credit for that?

COMMANDER IN CHIEF (*touching his epaulets*). You're jealous of these, aren't you?

KHLUDOV. You are the most extreme demonstration of how it's always the idiots who rise to the top, the most inept bumblers and bunglers who get promoted time after time.

I hate you because of your broken promises about help from the West and how many reserves we had. I hate you as a man hates when he is forced to act, yet he knows, day after day, how hopeless it all is and he'd be better off gardening or playing the piano in a brothel.

You were right this summer. I was sick – sick of you and I'm still sick of you and it's a great disappointment to feel no particular joy now it's finally sunk in that we're headed for oblivion together.

COMMANDER IN CHIEF. Why don't you stay here, then? That'll be your quickest route to oblivion.

KHLUDOV. I'm seriously thinking about it.

In exasperation the COMMANDER IN CHIEF *picks up a chair and starts to smash it.*

COMMANDER IN CHIEF. I made you sick? They made me those promises, too. How do you think I felt when every battle I trusted you with turned into a rout? But it won't be your name in the history books as the man who lost the Russian Empire, will it? Will it? It'll be mine. Mine. Mine.

KHLUDOV (*mildly*). Now would Alexander the Great have broken a chair like that?

COMMANDER IN CHIEF. One more word – just one more word –

A JUNIOR OFFICER rushes in through one of the doors, salutes.

JUNIOR OFFICER. The Commandant of the Cavalry School at Simferol is here for orders, sir.

Unable to trust himself any further, the COMMANDER IN CHIEF *rushes out through one door leaving* KHLUDOV *alone.* KHLUDOV *starts opening doors, closing them, opening more doors and looking out as if he's trying to find someone. As he's doing so the ghost of* KRAPILIN *walks on.*

When he sees him KHLUDOV *gives a long-suffering sigh.*

KHLUDOV. I gave you strict orders to stop pestering me. Do you want me to hang you again?

KRAPILIN. I never asked to be hung in the first place.

KHLUDOV. What do you expect me to do about it now? You had to open your mouth, you had to draw attention to yourself, didn't you? What could I do?

KRAPILIN. That's not for me to say, is it? The point is something's got to be done.

KHLUDOV. I can't unhang you, can I?

KRAPILIN. Not up to me, is it? I don't know the answer.

KHLUDOV. It was all for your own good anyway. You can't go around saying what you're thinking. What kind of mess would that get us all into?

A door opens and GOLUBKOV *rushes in, breathlessly determined to get it all off his chest.*

GOLUBKOV. There was nobody outside so I came right in. I wish to make a formal complaint against General Khludov, – kidnap, illegal imprisonment, rape too for all I know.

KHLUDOV. You again?

GOLUBKOV (*in shock*). Oh my God –

KHLUDOV. Help me with this. Did we hang you, too?

GOLUBKOV. Me? Hang me?

KHLUDOV (*to* KRAPILIN). Didn't we?

KRAPILIN. I've got my own problems. My feet hurt –

KHLUDOV. How in God's name can your feet hurt?

Unaware that KHLUDOV*'s talking to the invisible* KRAPILIN.

GOLUBKOV. Well, I've worn out three pairs of boots since I left St. Petersburg –

Unseen by him KRAPILIN *takes his boots off and massages his feet as* KHLUDOV *gives an explosive sign, turns back to* GOLUBKOV.

KHLUDOV. Remind me again –

GOLUBKOV. In the Crimea you had a woman arrested – I was arrested at the same time, so was her husband.

KHLUDOV. I remember now. They let you go? Splendid, I'm glad it ended so well. In the soup one day and out the next, that's the thing. (*To* KRAPILIN.) Put those boots back on straight away and stand at attention. You're still a soldier, remember that.

Flustered, GOLUBKOV *pulls himself upright, tries to look military as* KRAPILIN *walks out moodily towards the door.*

KRAPILIN. Am I? I wouldn't be so sure about that.

KHLUDOV. Wouldn't you? (*To* GOLUBKOV.) You're here to complain about me to the Commander in Chief?

GOLUBKOV. Yes.

KRAPILIN. No I wouldn't.

KHLUDOV. We'll see about that. (*To* GOLUBKOV.) Unfortunately he's gone plop. Fell off the edge of the table straight into a bucket of water, just like that.

KRAPILIN. Will we?

KHLUDOV. Fine figure of a man, splendid epaulets, remember him taking the salute at Tsarskoye Selo before this business started, sun shining on his silver buckles and now - plop, off the kitchen table. Tip tip tip tip tip plop, just like the rest of them. (*To* KRAPILIN.) Yes we will. (*To* GOLUBKOV.) My dear sir, I regret there is no one to complain to about General Khludov because there is no one to complain to about anything any longer –

KRAPILIN *leaves and there's the whizz and bang of a falling shell and an* ORDERLY *hurries in.*

ORDERLY. Firing on the outskirts of town, sir. The ships are leaving.

KHLUDOV. Very sensible, too. These naval men don't wait around. When the tide's right it's Up Anchor and off they go.

Do me a favour – pop over to the Counter Intelligence section and ask Tikhi if there's a woman name of –

GOLUBKOV. Korzukhin – Serafima Vladimitrovna Korzukhin.

KHLUDOV. Bring her here if she hasn't been shot.

ORDERLY. Shot?

KHLUDOV. That is, if she's in an un-shot condition, is that plainer?

The ORDERLY *leaves by one door as the listless* KRAPILIN *enters by another, whistling through his teeth.*

Only the idiots are left. Anyone with an ounce of sense has left days ago.

GOLUBKOV. If she's dead I'll kill you myself.

KHLUDOV (*eagerly*). That would be a splendid way out, that would solve everything, wouldn't it?

Beat.

No, it wouldn't work. You're a nice enough chap but you could never bring yourself to kill anyone.

It's a character flaw – but thank you for the offer –

(*To* KRAPILIN.) And stop that whistling.

GOLUBKOV. Whistling?

KRAPILIN. What's happening now, then?

KHLUDOV. Don't give me that accusing look all the time. I'm a very strong willed man, one ghost isn't going to knock me sideways. What next? Wailing? Chains?

GOLUBKOV. General – ?

KHLUDOV (*ignores him*). You don't have the imagination to carry this off, you're still what you were, one of the tens of thousands, millions, who fall under the wheels and never get up again.

KRAPILIN. I was following orders. Your orders.

KHLUDOV. If you had any sense you'd have deserted as soon as things started going badly.

KRAPILIN. Orders are orders.

GOLUBKOV (*totally confused*). Shall I wait outside?

KHLUDOV. Did I personally beg you to march into battle behind the regimental bands as if it was an Easter Parade? It's all very well to blame the Generals and Field Marshals when things go wrong – if the soldiers. disappeared at the first sign of trouble nobody would have anything to complain about, would they?

GOLUBKOV. That's a very good point –

KRAPILIN. My feet still hurt.

KHLUDOV. Shut up.

GOLUBKOV. Sir?

KRAPILIN. I've had nothing to eat for days.

KHLUDOV. I said shut up.

GOLUBKOV. Yes sir.

Turning abruptly back to GOLUBKOV.

KHLUDOV. What do you want?

GOLUBKOV. What do I want?

KHLUDOV. This woman you're looking for – your mistress?

GOLUBKOV. No, it hasn't come to that yet, exactly –

KHLUDOV. But you love her?

GOLUBKOV. Do I love her? Of course I love her, what else could explain it? But how do I know for sure? Yes, yes, I love her but sometimes I wish I'd never set eyes on her. I can't wait for that moment when I suddenly realize she's nobody special, she's too skinny, she's too fat, her eyes are too close together or they're too far apart and what a complete waste of time it's all been.

KHLUDOV. Do you want her or not? My head's splitting. First you're going to kill me for her, now you want rid of her.

KRAPILIN. My feet still hurt.

KHLUDOV. I told you to shut up.

KRAPILIN. You don't know how to speak to people.

KHLUDOV. You think this is funny, do you, hanging around here annoying me?

GOLUBKOV *heads to the door.*

GOLUBKOV. Do you want me to go?

KRAPILIN. I never asked to be hung.

KHLUDOV. Don't keep saying that. (*To* GOLUBKOV.) Come back here.

GOLUBKOV. You want me to stay?

KHLUDOV (*to* KRAPILIN). You do, I suppose?

KRAPILIN. Do what?

KHLUDOV. Know how to speak to people.

KRAPILIN. The girl. You remember her, don't you?

KHLUDOV (*to* KRAPILIN). You were a damn fool before and you'll be a damn fool to the end of time, however long that is.

He barks a laugh and heads out, leaving KRAPILIN *leaning on the wall, rubbing his feet.*

GOLUBKOV. My darling Serafima, how odd that I never noticed that Khludov was out of his mind. I just accepted it – the bodies, the idiocies.

KRAPILIN. He'll be back.

GOLUBKOV. Maybe I will kill him. It doesn't seem such a big decision, suddenly.

KRAPILIN. He's not well, you know –

GOLUBKOV. But if I kill him, I'll be killing a madman, so what would be the point? And how would I do it? That's one of the problems of not being a practical man. Where to aim? No amount of philosophy can make up for a week in a slaughterhouse or a day helping the public executioner.

KRAPILIN. Not well at all.

Another door opens and KHLUDOV *walks in again, a hopeful expression on his face. He thrusts his pistol into the startled* GOLUBKOV's *hand.*

KHLUDOV (*encouragingly*). You might shoot, you never can tell. Worried? Blaze away, I've taken the safety catch off.

GOLUBKOV. I can't, no, I'm sorry.

KHLUDOV. Quite sure?

KRAPILIN. Sure?

GOLUBKOV. Positive.

KHLUDOV. Oh well, some other time, perhaps – (*To* KRAPILIN.) It would have settled your hash though, wouldn't it?

He takes the pistol back, drops his voice, confidential.

You know what the problem's been? We've all been play-acting. Everybody except the Bolsheviks, they knew what they wanted all along.

The door opens and a rattled SKUNSKY *comes in.*

SKUNSKY. General Khludov?

KHLUDOV. What is it?

SKUNSKY *has left the door open and* KRAPILIN *yawns, scratches himself and stands looking out through it.*

SKUNSKY. Did you send an Orderly to check on the whereabouts of a woman named – hang on, I've got it here somewhere –

He feels in his pockets.

I could swear I had it.

GOLUBKOV. Korzukhin, Serafima Vladimitrovna Korzukhin –

KRAPILIN. Something like that –

SKUNSKY. That was it, yes, thank you – sorry to be a nuisance.

He's heading out again when GOLUBKOV *stops him.*

GOLUBKOV. What's happened to her?

KHLUDOV. The point is where's my Orderly?

SKUNSKY. You can guess what it's like at Counter Intelligence at the moment, General – somebody pops up out of the blue asking where this person or that person is – well, we have to be careful.

KHLUDOV. Where is my Orderly?

SKUNSKY. We shot him. But it's all right, now we know he was who he said he was.

GOLUBKOV. The woman, Serafima, where is she?

KHLUDOV (*ignoring him*). Send Tikhi to me, there's been too much of this kind of thing.

SKUNSKY. Hung himself, General, from the pipes in the basement of Counter Intelligence.

Near breaking point GOLUBKOV *steps between them.*

GOLUBKOV. Where is Serafima Vladimitrovna Korzukhin?

SKUNSKY. On the SS Vitazy with General Charnota.

KHLUDOV. So Charnota's gone, too? Then it really is over.

Through the sound of the shells we hear again the playing of CHARNOTA's *Brass Band. They all incline their heads, listening to it until it fades and dies away completely.*

A waltz, wasn't it?

GOLUBKOV. Where's the ship headed?

SKUNSKY. Constantinople.

GOLUBKOV. She's safe?

SKUNSKY. There's still a file open – now that poor old Tikhi's cashed in his chips, it's Joe Muggins here who'll have to pick up the pieces, I suppose.

KHLUDOV. It's over, you bloody fool.

KRAPILIN (*to* GOLUBKOV). He just can't talk to people.

KHLUDOV *indicates the window.*

KHLUDOV. What do you see out there? Ship after ship steaming away, the decks filled with defeated men and the holds filled with everything they've been able to loot. It's over. It's the end of the road.

Artillery starts to boom in the distance.

Hear that? Everything, everybody smashed to pieces for once and for all in one glorious, tremendous, amazing and in some ways utterly wonderful smash.

SKUNSKY. What do we do now, General?

KHLUDOV (*to* GOLUBKOV). Always the same question, isn't it? Have you noticed that?

SKUNSKY. Where do we go?

KHLUDOV. And that's always the next question and the answer is always so damned obvious.

Spinning SKUNSKY *around to face away from the window.*

Russia. The Bolsheviks. The Red Army.

Spinning him around in the other direction.

Constantinople.

He spins him round again.

Come with me. We'll make one last stand. When the Reds arrive at least we'll go down fighting.

GOLUBKOV. I'm not sure I like the sound of that.

KRAPILIN. I don't like the sound of it at all.

KHLUDOV. Left! Right! Left right left! –

He marches KRAPILIN *to the door, calls to* SKUNSKY.

You too –

SKUNSKY. Oh bloody hell –

He unknowingly falls in line behind KRAPILIN.

KHLUDOV. What about you? She's gone and that's it. She never cared for you anyway, did she?

GOLUBKOV. I'll come with you. Let's end it like it should be ended, with a bullet in the head or a sword point in the heart.

KHLUDOV. That's the spirit.

At the door his nerve fails him again.

GOLUBKOV. Or perhaps to have my arm ripped off or lie there for hours with my stomach torn open, begging for water.

KHLUDOV. Make up your mind. Are you coming or aren't you?

GOLUBKOV. You promise it'll be quick?

KHLUDOV. We don't stand a chance. It'll be over in minutes, ask anyone who knows my Generalship.

He marches KRAPILIN *and* SKUNSKY *off, leaving* GOLUBKOV *alone. On the way out something snags his memory.*

GOLUBKOV. That lampshade . . . a little fringe. Tassels. And a brass base.

Pleased at having restored the complete, private memory, he heads off as the sound of muezzins calling the faithful to prayer mixes with the whizz and bang of crashing shells, the hooting of ship's sirens and the very last distant echoes of CHARNOTA's *brass band.*

A dust cover falls from the ceiling and covers everything and it's the –

End of the Fourth Dream.

Fifth Dream

The lights rise to the cry from a muezzin. We're in a strange mix of East and West now – under the shadow of the mosque HOOKERS *ply their trade from barred windows or dark doorways,* BRITISH SAILORS *on shore leave stagger from bar to bar or sprawl on the ground, sodden in drink.*

Through the crowd weaves CHARNOTA, *wearing his begrimed Cossack uniform minus epaulets, holding a score of inflated balloons for sale.*

He's no longer the charming, urbane officer – the travails of exile have taken a bitter toll on his manners, speech and outlook.

CHARNOTA. Balloons, balloons for the kiddies, nice balloons, get your nice balloons here, any colour you like –

A veiled TURKISH WOMAN *walks past him.*

CHARNOTA. Madame – achetez pour votre enfant –

TURKISH WOMAN. Bybun fiya ty nadyr? Combien?

CHARNOTA. Cinquante piastres, Madame, cinquante.

TURKISH WOMAN. Oh yokh! Bu pakhali dyr!

She sweeps past him, despite his protests.

CHARNOTA. Forty, Madame, only forty piastres –

Gives up.

Oh bugger off then, back to the harem you fat old cow.

Jesus Christ, what a filthy hole this town is. Constantinople? Jewel of the East? Arse end of the Universe, more like.

Shouts after her.

Forty piastres? For a balloon like this? Screw you and the family eunuch, too!

Approaching a group of BRITISH SAILORS.

Rule Britannia! God save the King!

BRITISH SAILOR. Fuck off you Turkish bastard –

CHARNOTA. I am a Russian officer, and Winston Churchill fucky fucks his grandmother.

The man drunkenly launches himself at him and **CHARNOTA** *is knocked to the ground and kicked and pummelled by him and his irate companions. When they head away he pulls himself to his feet and heads for a large board with two squares cut in it.*

Dusting himself down, he heads to the board and raps on a window. A window shoots open and **ATHANASIUS** *sticks his head out.*

ATHANASIUS. What?

CHARNOTA. What's the favourite on the five o'clock, Archbishop?

ATHANASIUS. Janissary, and I keep telling you, I'm not an Archbishop any more.

CHARNOTA. A hundred piastres to win, I'll pay you out of my winnings. Quick, before Lyuska sees me.

ATHANASIUS. Yanko Yankovich!

The second window slams open and **DE BRISARD** *sticks his head out in his new identity as* **YANKO YANKOVITCH.**

YANKO. What?

CHARNOTA. My dear de Brisard –

YANKO. No.

The window slams down and **CHARNOTA** *raps on it until it opens again.*

YANKO. What?

CHARNOTA. You didn't let me finish.

YANKO. No, I didn't let you start and the answer's still No. No credit to anyone, especially Russians. And the name is Yankovitch.

CHARNOTA. Balloon? Any colour you like.

The window slams shut in his face again.

ATHANASIUS. There's a bug on your face, Grigory Lukyanich.

CHARNOTA. Good. If I let it mind its own business, maybe somebody will let me mind mine.

Mopping his brow from the heat.

Jesus Christ, what a dump. I thought I'd crawled all over the armpits of the world in my time but this – fat cows in veils, being told to Fuck Off in ten different languages –

Sighs.

Kharkov now, there's a city – Rostov – Kiev – that's a beautiful place, Kiev – the monastery on top of the hill, the sun shining on it. The Dneiper – oh God, the Dneiper, the light, indescribable. The smell of grass, the smell of hay, the hills and the valleys as shapely as a young girl, the barges going up and down, up and down all day long.

He starts to scratch himself, searching his clothes for lice.

The louse – now there's an insect for you –

ATHANASIUS. Don't be disgusting.

CHARNOTA. My dear man, you'll never be able to savour to the full the joys of exile if you can't differentiate between insects.

There's a lot to be said for the louse – he's tough, virile, gives as good as he gets. It's a fair fight with a louse. He's a military man in his own way, he's got his infantry and his cavalry, his frontal assaults and his ambushes, always keeps plenty of men in reserve, never knows when he's beaten –

Not like your bedbug, who's just a parasite, a civilian, lazing round in pyjamas all day, like yourself, Archbishop.

Suddenly he bangs on the second window again and YANKO *looks out, tugging a dinner jacket and bow tie into place.*

YANKO. What now?

CHARNOTA. I've got a business proposition for you. I've been thinking of getting out of the balloon line and I'm prepared to give you first refusal. What do you say?

YANKO. Fifty piastres for the lot.

CHARNOTA. Don't be ridiculous. These balloons sell for fifty each and even at that price I can't get enough of them to keep up with demand.

YANKO. Good, then you'll die a rich man.

He slams the window shut as CHARNOTA *makes a throat slitting gesture.*

CHARNOTA. Is that any way for a Russian officer to treat another one? When I think of all the fighting I did in the Crimea, holding the rearguard –

ATHANASIUS. Don't you mean running?

CHARNOTA. And what were you doing? Where was the Church when we needed it?

ATHANASIUS. I carry my faith inside me. Where's yours? Do you have any left? In anything?

Before CHARNOTA *can answer the window goes up again.*

YANKO. A hundred and fifty piastres for everything.

CHARNOTA. May you rot in hell – as if we aren't already there – it's a deal.

He pushes the balloons through the window.

A hundred and fifty on Janissary in the five o'clock.

YANKO *steps out in front of the board, buttoning up his dinner jacket as he raises an Imperial flag from a pole.* ATHANASIUS *takes out his cross and beats it with a metal bar to drum up business among the* BRITISH SAILORS *and others who cluster around the stall.*

YANKO. Messieurs, mesdames, les courses commencent. Please place your bets. The favourite pastime of the court of the late Tsar and Tsarina, never before seen outside the walls of the Imperial Residences.

CHARNOTA. Get on with it –

ATHANASIUS. A little bit of Old Russia before your very eyes. The game played on the morning of the execution of the Tsar and all his family. L'amusement preféré de la défunte imperatrice!

CHARNOTA. This is disgusting – they've hardly shovelled the poor man and his family into the ground and listen to yourself –

YANKO (*ignoring him*). Place your bets now –

ATHANASIUS *sets a flat board on an upturned crate as* YANKO *flips open a folding step ladder and climbs onto it.* ATHANASIUS *starts taking small black objects from a box and setting them carefully on the board.*

YANKO. The runners in tonight's first race are Number One – Black Pearl, Number Two – the favourite Janissary, Number Three – Baba Yaga, Number Four – a gray cockroach with white spots, Don't Cry Baby, Number Five – Hooligan and Number Six – Buttons.

You will observe that the cockroaches run on open planks in plain view with paper jockeys. There is absolutely no opportunity for any deceit or sleight of hand. Not to be confused with inferior copies, these are the genuine and original Cockroach Derbies of Old Istanbul –

CHARNOTA. Yes yes yes, get on with it –

ATHANASIUS. Weighed in!

YANKO. The cockroaches are selected from the finest specimens in Europe and live in a sealed box under the personal supervision of a Professor of Entomology from Kazan Imperial University, just escaped from the Bolsheviks.

CHARNOTA. That's new. That's a nice touch.

ATHANASIUS. Under Starter's Orders!

Bending over the board, YANKO *keeps up a commentary as* CHARNOTA *and the others urge their bets on.*

YANKO. Black Pearl is first away, followed by Don't Cry, Baby with Janissary and Hooligan showing strong and Buttons a slow starter. Baba Yaga nowhere as Janissary starts to fade too –

CHARNOTA. Damn –

ATHANASIUS *takes up the commentary.*

ATHANASIUS. Buttons comes up on the outside as Don't Cry starts to go back, Baby rallies and Hooligan and Buttons pass Janissary who's showing no form at all and with three lengths to go it's Black Pearl and Buttons –

YANKO. Black Pearl and Buttons neck and neck and Janissary runs out as up with the leaders it's Black Pearl and Buttons, Buttons and Black Pearl, neck and neck and it's Black Pearl by a length –

The few winners cheer and are paid out as the others head away grumbling, leaving a stunned CHARNOTA *behind.*

CHARNOTA. What happened to Janissary?

YANKO. It's not the first time the favourite failed to come through.

CHARNOTA. It's the first time the favourite's rolled on his back and kicked his legs in the air.

Suspiciously, he picks the cockroach up despite YANKO's *objections, sniffs it.*

CHARNOTA. Beer. I can smell beer.

YANKO. Cockroaches don't drink beer.

CHARNOTA. They do if it's given to them.

YANKO. When have you seen a drunken cockroach?

He grabs it back and hands it to ATHANASIUS *as*
CHARNOTA *shakes his head.*

CHARNOTA. I bet on the long shots, they run backwards. I bet on
the favourite, he's a cockroach dipsomaniac. And why is he the
favourite anyway? Because you say so. You decide he's the
favourite because you know I'm tired of betting at sixty to one
and today I'll try the favourite for once.

YANKO. That's the turf for you. (*To* ATHANASIUS.) Get them
ready for the five fifteen. There's another British warship just
arrived.

CHARNOTA. Isn't it time somebody told them they bet on the
wrong horse, too?

A heavy sigh.

Well that's it, Yanko. You've finally done it – cleaned me out
completely. In six weeks you've turned me into a gambler and
a pauper. Well done.

YANKO. There's always your boots.

CHARNOTA. You're not getting my boots.

YANKO. Such nice boots. Cavalry boots, such wonderful Russian
leather, stout soles, look at those laces –

CHARNOTA. You've got the heart of a poet, Yanko. 'The Imperial
Majesty's favourite game' –

YANKO. You like that? No hard feelings?

CHARNOTA. None at all, even though I've often thought it would
have been more honest to have hit me on the head and gone
through my pockets the first time you saw me.

YANKO. I didn't ask you to bet, did I?

CHARNOTA. Then lend me the money. You'll get it back, you
know you will.

YANKO. That would be impossible, quite impossible. That would
be charity and you're too proud a man to accept charity, isn't
he, Archbishop?

CHARNOTA. Proud? What in God's name have I to be proud of?
What have any of us to be proud of?

YANKO *starts chalking up prices for the next race as*
CHARNOTA *turns to* ATHANASIUS.

Aren't you ashamed of yourself, making your living like this?

ATHANASIUS. It won't be for long.

He drops his voice to a confidential whisper.

Have you seen how many cats there are here? Thousands of them. All it takes is 'Here moggy moggy' and a sharp knife and you're in the fur coat business. Want to come in on it with me?

CHARNOTA. I'm a soldier, not a furrier.

ATHANASIUS. You're a balloon seller, without any balloons.

CHARNOTA. I can't learn the trick of it, somehow, living like this. Here's you with your furs and Yanko with his blasted cockroach races and Lyuska –

ATHANASIUS. She seems to have settled in.

CHARNOTA. What do you mean by that? What are you trying to say? What's that supposed to mean?

Furious, he grabs him by the cross hung around his neck, twists it tight as YANKO *climbs onto the step ladder again and starts pitching the next race.*

YANKO. Mesdames, messieurs, place your bets for the five fifteen. Six pure bred cockroaches will run on a measured course under conditions of the strictest security –

The Lights get brighter and brighter, flooding the stage with an intense and dazzling white light as a half dozen muezzins chant earsplittingly loudly, their cries mingling with YANKO's *as he prepares for the next race.*

The crowd drifts away – CHARNOTA *seems to be the only potential punter in sight.*

YANKO. The runners in the five fifteen are Number One – Heart's Desire, Number Two – the favourite Topaz, Number Three – Up and Running, Number Four – Sweet Dreams, Number Five – Lover Boy and Number Six – Rainbow's End.

Once again ATHANASIUS *starts taking small black objects from a box and setting them carefully on the board.*

ATHANASIUS. Weighed in! Place your bets, please – this is the final race on this evening's card –

CHARNOTA *hesitates, helpless in the face of the temptation to gamble yet again, even though he's the only gambler.*

CHARNOTA. It's a trick, that's what it is. You go to bed a Russian one night and you wake up next morning and you're Yanko Yankovich or in the fur trade or like Lyuska – (*To* YANKO.) How much for the boots?

YANKO. Five hundred piastres.

CHARNOTA. Who's the favourite?

YANKO. Topaz.

CHARNOTA. Five hundred on Topaz to win.

ATHANASIUS. Under starter's orders!

> CHARNOTA *gives a heavy sigh as he looks down at his boots, as if saying farewell to them.*

CHARNOTA. Kiev – ? Now Kiev was a battle, that really was a beautiful fight. Perfect weather - warm, sunny but not too hot, everything you need –

YANKO. They're off!

> *In dead silence he walks along the race track then stops dead as his bet pulls up. He takes off his boots slowly as the muezzins' calls get louder and shriller.*

> *End of the Fifth Dream.*

Sixth Dream

The blinding white light fades to a garish pink glow of evening as a barefoot CHARNOTA *heads for a squalid house in a Constantinople back street.*

LYUSKA *is waiting for him.*

LYUSKA. Here she comes – Madame Barabanchikova, the Balloon Queen of Constantinople. So she's finally agreed to sell her boots? Thank God for that – Serafima and I haven't eaten since yesterday morning.

How much did you get for them?

CHARNOTA. It's not as simple as that. I took the balloons and my silver cartridge pockets and my boots to the Grand Bazaar and, well, I turned my back and –

LYUSKA. Don't tell me – they were stolen?

CHARNOTA. In an instant, in a flash they were gone, just like that.

LYUSKA. The man with the thick black beard took them, I suppose?

CHARNOTA. I didn't get a good look at the thief –

LYUSKA. Yes, it was probably the man with the thick black beard – the same one who stole the candlesticks from you last week and the Icon of the Virgin and all my lace the week before that.

Really, Madame Barabanchikova, you should be much more careful when you see him following you. When you finally have that baby you'll only have to turn your back for a moment and he'll be off with it.

CHARNOTA. Don't call me a liar and don't call me Madame Barabanchikova.

LYUSKA. I bought those balloons with my own money – and you know what I had to do to earn it.

CHARNOTA (*hastily*). That's your business.

LYUSKA. It's my business when I disappear for twenty minutes with a Frenchman or a soldier or a British sailor – it's your

business and your money when I bring it back, yours and
Serafima's –

Unseen by them, SERAFIMA *enters with a pile of laundry,
listens to the argument.*

CHARNOTA. The balloon business has been rather slow, I admit.

LYUSKA. The cockroaches have been even slower, that's the
problem. That's where everything went, wasn't it?

A sigh, a remnant of her previous love for him showing.

Grisha, Grisha, how could you do it? You got cashiered from
the army for smashing up the Counter Intelligence Head
Quarters and now we're all going to starve to death in
Constantinople.

CHARNOTA. I saved Serafima Vladimitrovna from being shot.
Doesn't that count for something?

LYUSKA. I'm very happy for her. She can keep on pining for
Korzukhin while living off the whore the pair of you have
made me.

SERAFIMA. Lyuska! –

A shrug from LYUSKA, *past caring.*

LYUSKA. It's very bad manners to eavesdrop.

SERAFIMA. I couldn't help overhearing and I didn't know how
you were making the money. I'll pay it back, every piastre.

LYUSKA. Wonderful. While you're at it, get him his job back, put
the Tsar back on the throne and make the Bolsheviks say how
sorry they are.

Suddenly angry.

Tomorrow the Greek is going to throw us out of this rat hole.
We have no money. There is no food in the house. And now
Madame Barabanchikova has even gambled away her balloons.

CHARNOTA. Put yourself in my place. I'm a soldier – how can I
be expected to turn myself into something useful just like that?
Balloons – dear God in heaven – balloons.

A hesitation.

How many then? How many have you slept with?

LYUSKA. Well, let's see – take the number of ships in the harbour
times the number of sailors on them –

CHARNOTA. No no, I can't bear it.

LYUSKA. Really? But you used to be a soldier, Madame.

SERAFIMA. Please don't call him that, Lyuska.

LYUSKA. Mind your own business.

SERAFIMA. It's my business if you sell yourself to feed me.

LYUSKA. I'm a whore now, understand? It's that or starve. Any principles I had flew out of the window when we got off the boat and I realized how big a mess we were in.

SERAFIMA. I can't have principles while you're on the streets for me. If that's what we have to do to get by – I'm coming with you next time.

LYUSKA. There'd be no need for either of us to go whoring if Madame would only agree to sell her revolver.

CHARNOTA. I'll sell my shirt, my pants, everything but don't ask me to give up my revolver. I may be a louse with it but without it I'm just a bed bug.

LYUSKA. All right – keep your revolver and live off what we earn. At least pimping's a profession.

Goaded beyond endurance he raises his fist but she doesn't move.

LYUSKA. Lay a hand on me and I'll poison you.

CHARNOTA. You mean there is something to eat?

LYUSKA. No, but I'll poison you as soon as there is.

Dumping the laundry on the side of the small fountain in the centre of the courtyard.

SERAFIMA. I can't stand it, I'm going out.

LYUSKA. Where?

SERAFIMA (*despairing*). Balloons, boots, our bodies – what does it matter what we sell?

LYUSKA. You wouldn't know how to start.

Heading for the door, defiant.

SERAFIMA. Paramon was a wonderful lover. He showed me everything that it takes to make a man happy.

LYUSKA. Against a wall? In a back street in Constantinople? With his drunken mates waiting for their turn? How far sighted of him.

CHARNOTA. Say another word and I'll shoot you.

LYUSKA (*to* SERAFIMA). What are you waiting for?

From somewhere in the tangle of back streets a barrel organ plays. A sigh from LYUSKA.

Come back, Serafima. You don't have to do this.

SERAFIMA. No, I don't suppose I do. But I'm going to.

She leaves as CHARNOTA *makes a half hearted protest.*

CHARNOTA. Serafima, come back – I forbid you –

She doesn't even turn back and he sits miserably beside the laundry.

LYUSKA. Congratulations. Now you've got both of us whoring for you.

CHARNOTA. I can confidently say I've never hated a place more than Constantinople, nor a woman more than you.

LYUSKA. I hate you. I hate myself. I hate all Russians. I'd stab myself only you've gambled away the knives and forks. I'd hang myself only you'd probably charge admission to see the body and spend it all on the cockroach races.

Picking up the laundry, she heads inside, leaving him to muse by himself.

CHARNOTA. Madrid? Spain, now – no, I bet that's a filthy hole, too. London? Ugh. Paris? Too disgusting for words. Berlin? Bed bugs everywhere.

Reaching down he picks up a cigarette butt.

That Greek is beyond belief the meanest son of a bitch I've ever come across. Who in God's name smokes a cigarette so far down to the butt? It's all right to say you hate Russians but we're not mean.

Carefully lighting the butt.

Athens? I bet that's an open sewer. Rome? That must be the filthiest of the lot.

GOLUBKOV *heads into the yard, turning the handle of the barrel organ.*

You there –

He pulls out the pistol and aims it at him.

I particularly hate barrel organs –

Recognizing GOLUBKOV.

Is that you, Sergei Golubkov?

GOLUBKOV. General Charnota – I've found you at last.

CHARNOTA. Another turn of the handle and you'd be dead.

He puts his gun away and they embrace.

We thought the Reds had got you, or Counter Intelligence had finished you off.

A closer look.

You look terrible.

GOLUBKOV. You don't look well yourself.

CHARNOTA. I'm a civilian now, slight difference of opinion with the Commander in Chief.

Pulling back slightly.

I hate to say it after all you look as if you've been through but, well – a barrel organ?

GOLUBKOV. I don't give a damn about it but the point is that with a barrel organ I can get to places I can't without it.

CHARNOTA. Meetings of barrel organ owners?

GOLUBKOV. One can wander the streets like a Troubadour, people let you inside their courtyards without throwing stones at you or wanting to shoot you – most of them.

Anxious.

I met Khludov in Sebastopol. He wasn't lying, was he? Serafima is still alive? You did save her from Counter Intelligence?

CHARNOTA. I did and in about ten minutes she'll be here.

GOLUBKOV. She will?

CHARNOTA. She'll be sucking off her first client about now and headed home.

GOLUBKOV. What are you talking about?

CHARNOTA. That may be putting it bluntly but there's no point beating about the bush. We're at rock bottom.

GOLUBKOV. She's on the streets? You put her on the streets?

CHARNOTA. Calm down. It's not my fault, I had nothing to do with it. Girls will be girls. We're dying of hunger, my horses aren't running at all, Lyuska's taken to calling me Madame Barabanchikova –

GOLUBKOV. Lyuska's here, too? You put her on the streets as well?

CHARNOTA. No. Yes – well, in a way. Damn it, I'm beginning to sound like you.

GOLUBKOV. This is awful.

CHARNOTA. That's only the start of it.

We're about to be evicted by a Greek who'd rather burn a hole in his lip than leave you with a butt worth smoking and I bet my cavalry boots on the five fifteen with winter coming on.

With a sad, puzzled sigh.

I just can't seem to get the hang of it, you see. The trick. You now, let's take a close look – (*Staring into his eyes. Relieved.*) No. It's not just me. You don't look as if you've got a clue, either.

(*Confidential.*) You're an educated man – what do you know about Madrid? I've been dreaming about Spain but if it's as filthy a hole as this –

He stops as, head bowed, SERAFIMA *heads into the court yard followed by an amorous* GREEK, *laden down with wine and groceries.*

SERAFIMA. Here we are, not all that far at all, was it? You did remember the cheese? And the bread? We'll have some of that thick coffee you all seem to like, have a nice talk and get to know each other and then –

She sees CHARNOTA, *takes a deep breath.*

SERAFIMA. Well, you see, I've made a start.

Stepping forward with a puzzled, uneasy smile.

GOLUBKOV. Serafima?

SERAFIMA. No music, thank you.

She looks more closely .

It's you?

GOLUBKOV. It's me, yes. Sergei Golubkov. I've finally found you.

SERAFIMA. And I thought the worst that could happen to me had happened.

Pointing at the Greek, encumbered with parcels.

GOLUBKOV. Who is this man?

SERAFIMA (*to* CHARNOTA). At the monastery, at the railway station, in Counter Intelligence Head Quarters, at the worst moments of my life I can rely on him to turn up like a nightmare and make things even worse. How does he do it and what have I done to deserve it?

GOLUBKOV. Who is he?

GREEK. Now, excuse me please, we go fucky fuck?

GOLUBKOV. Oh My God. Is that what it's come to?

CHARNOTA. I warned you, didn't I?

GOLUBKOV suddenly hits the GREEK in the chest. The surprised man sprawls backwards in the dirt.

GOLUBKOV. Do you think I might borrow your gun for a moment, General?

CHARNOTA. I'd grant most things to someone who still called me General but I think he's had enough. (*To* GREEK.) No fucky fuck. Not today. But you can leave the bread and cheese behind.

He pulls him to his feet and pushes him out of the courtyard as GOLUBKOV winces at the pain in his fist. LYUSKA comes out of the house, listens.

GOLUBKOV. It hurts. Maybe I've broken it. How do people batter other people senseless when one punch hurts so much? It puts the beatings I've had in a completely new light – but of course it's very hard to pay attention when you're flying off the walls and trying to work out where they're going to hit you next and what you can do, if anything, to stop them –

LYUSKA. God, he's back.

SERAFIMA. Yes, he's back.

LYUSKA. He didn't have the barrel organ before, did he?

SERAFIMA. No, that's new.

LYUSKA. Another useless mouth to feed.

GOLUBKOV. I can explain all about that statement –

LYUSKA. Well, how did it go? Did you pick anyone up?

SERAFIMA. A Greek, but The Nightmare beat him up and Charnota stole his bread and cheese. So I'll have to go out and do it all over again tomorrow.

Still rubbing his knuckles –

GOLUBKOV. Serafima Vladimitrovna Korzukhin – for six months I've been looking for you, practising the words I was going to say to you, falling asleep pretending I was holding you in my arms –

SERAFIMA. From now on that kind of thing is strictly cash down, first come, first served.

GOLUBKOV. I'm going mad – how can you say that?

SERAFIMA. I'm going mad – how can you keep persecuting me?

GOLUBKOV. I don't even want anything from you, just to look at you again.

SERAFIMA. Bread, cheese, wine, salami – that's all I care about now. When it comes down to it, what else is there?

GOLUBKOV. Don't I mean anything to you?

SERAFIMA. God – Oh God –

She heads to the doorway and he follows, dazed and despairing.

GOLUBKOV. Where are you going?

SERAFIMA. Don't follow me. I never want to see you again. Do you understand? I want nothing to do with you. I don't want the worst moments of my life being made even worse by your stupidity.

She's gone and he's left staring at the gate, his dreams of their reunion shattered.

GOLUBKOV. Is that it? She's gone? Just like that?

LYUSKA. Looks like it. Got the message, have you? And don't waste your time trying to follow her.

Taking CHARNOTA *by surprise, he wrests the gun from him.*

GOLUBKOV. I'll kill her –

Stopping even before he gets to the gate.

GOLUBKOV. Khludov was right, I don't have the moral fibre to kill anyone.

LYUSKA. Have some bread and cheese. You'll see it all differently then.

GOLUBKOV. Absolutely not. I'd choke on it. Think what she was going to have to do to earn it.

LYUSKA. It's not so bad, after the first time. I wouldn't say you get used to it but there are worse things and you have to eat, don't you?

CHARNOTA. That's an appalling attitude. Golubkov's right. (*At* GOLUBKOV.) You're absolutely right. One has to make a stand somewhere.

He takes the food and dumps it into the fountain.

GOLUBKOV. A magnificent gesture, General. I haven't eaten for three days but well done.

LYUSKA. Well that's it, Madame Barabanchikova – I wish you good luck with the confinement and hope you're back on your feet as soon as possible. I'm going to the railway station.

CHARNOTA. To throw yourself in front of a train, I hope?

LYUSKA. The driver. And the fireman. And the guard. And as many of the passengers as it takes to screw my way across Europe.

Why in God's name did I waste six months of my life in this place with you?

CHARNOTA *grabs the gun back from* GOLUBKOV.

CHARNOTA. I'll kill you.

LYUSKA. A woman in your condition?

CHARNOTA. I'll shoot you and kill myself.

LYUSKA. You can't shoot me any more than he could shoot Serafima.

CHARNOTA. You said you'd stay with me, go anywhere with me.

A deep breath, his shoulders slumping.

I'll let you go, if that's what you want, but just once, before you leave – call me General again.

LYUSKA. At the point of a gun?

Shamefaced, he lowers it.

Goodbye, Madame.

GOLUBKOV *wrestles the gun away from him as with a roar, the maddened* CHARNOTA *tries to shoot her. Laughing,* LYUSKA *runs out of the gate.* CHARNOTA *stops, shrugs, lets her go, defeated and deflated.*

CHARNOTA. She's right. It was a stupid thing to do. a gesture's a gesture but a loaf of bread –

He fishes the bread and cheese out of the well and starts to chew on it.

Well? What are you going to do? Are you going to follow her or not?

GOLUBKOV. I can't face another day of that barrel organ. I had a monkey once, you know, until it bit me on the arm –

CHARNOTA. Can't you just eat?

GOLUBKOV. What about the principle?

CHARNOTA. Serafima's right – bread, wine, cheese, salami, that's what it boils down to, it takes a woman to know these things.

A hesitation, then GOLUBKOV *reaches for the bread, takes a bite.*

GOLUBKOV. You know, this cheese is really rather good.

Throwing his principles aside he starts to eat as hungrily as CHARNOTA *as* KHLUDOV *enters, tattered but still erect. When he sees him* CHARNOTA *drops what he's eating, pulls himself to his full height, snaps off a salute.*

CHARNOTA. Roman –

KHLUDOV. I keep telling you to stop making that foolish military gesture, Charnota. The war's lost and there's nothing more ridiculous than a losing general unless it's two losing generals.

Turning to look behind him.

KHLUDOV. Oh God, where's he got to now? (*Bellowing out through the gate.*) Hallo! Here we are!. Top of the hill! Pick those feet up! Left, right, left, left, left, right, left –

GOLUBKOV. General Khludov – I thought you were going to make a last stand in Sebastopol.

KHLUDOV. So were you.

GOLUBKOV. I got lost. Then I got very sick and then they put me in prison and I got sick again and they let me go and ever since then I've been trying to find my way here, on foot.

KHLUDOV. What a contemptible thing this hunger for life is, the craving for one more day, then another one – and why should a man be any different just because he's wearing a General's uniform?

Beat.

You've met up with her again, then? That woman?

GOLUBKOV. Don't ask me anything about her.

KHLUDOV. A boy, a girl, a barrel organ – very Russian.

The weary KRAPILIN enters, leans against a wall, getting his breath back. KHLUDOV takes no notice of him.

How did it go?

GOLUBKOV. She's – she's –

CHARNOTA. She's out whoring, like that bitch Lyuska.

GOLUBKOV. You shouldn't speak of Lyuska like that.

CHARNOTA (*despairing*). It's just that I can't learn the trick, you see, every morning I wake up and I think it's all going to be just like it was, shabby and ridiculous, yes, it might have been at times but there was something about it, don't you think?

KRAPILIN. I know what he means. That's just what I feel.

KHLUDOV. Shut up.

KRAPILIN. Don't you feel it, too? You do, don't you?

KHLUDOV. You've no business talking to me like that.

KRAPILIN. You've no business bringing me here. You had no right to hang me in the first place.

KHLUDOV. Back to that, are we?

CHARNOTA. Roman – please.

KHLUDOV (*to* GOLUBKOV). It's not much of a place, Constantinople, and there are far too many Russians here but Lyuska and Serafima take care of us –

Seeing the food, he starts to eat.

KHLUDOV. You see? I really don't know how they manage it.

GOLUBKOV (*with sudden decisiveness*). I've made up my mind. I'm going to Paris to look for Korzukhin. He must be worth a fortune by now. I'll tell him she needs money. I won't even tell her that it was me who made him pay up, in case she throws it back at me –

KHLUDOV. Do you have the fare to Paris?

GOLUBKOV. I'll stow away on a boat. If I can't, I'll walk – there's only six or seven countries in the way.

KHLUDOV. That's the attitude, that's what we want. There's a lesson there. Too late to apply it now, of course, but there it is.

CHARNOTA. Paris – from all one has read it seems an abominable place. Granted, there isn't much to be said for Constantinople but you can always tell yourself that Russia's not so far away –

GOLUBKOV. I'm leaving. I'm going now.

A shrug from CHARNOTA, *completely reversing his position.*

CHARNOTA. Well – one should be prepared to try anything.

I'll come with you.

GOLUBKOV. Who'll keep an eye on Serafima?

CHARNOTA. Khludov, of course. What else is he good for?

GOLUBKOV. You think he's up to it?

CHARNOTA. A man who once ruled half of Russia?

With his newly discovered firmness GOLUBKOV *breaks the news to* KHLUDOV.

GOLUBKOV. We're both going to Paris – Charnota and me. I want you to swear to keep looking for Serafima and see that no harm comes to her.

CHARNOTA *makes sure that* KHLUDOV *gets it, speaking to him like a deaf man or a child.*

CHARNOTA. You'll find her in the bazaar with a male friend or two. You understand?

KHLUDOV. Oh dear, it's come to that, has it?

CHARNOTA. Make sure nothing happens to her.

KHLUDOV. Nobody's ever got away from Roman Khludov but why, exactly, should I make her my responsibility?

A shrug.

Very well, I'll do it.

Here, take this silver medallion –

He takes a piece of silver from his watch chain.

This might keep you going.

Reaching for the barrel organ.

You won't be needing this?

GOLUBKOV. It's yours.

KHLUDOV. Now if I only had a monkey.

CHARNOTA. You don't need one. Golubkov had one once and it bit him in the balls –

KHLUDOV. My God –

Running his hand over the barrel organ.

What do you do?

GOLUBKOV. Turn the handle, it's perfectly simple –

KHLUDOV *does so and beams as the music floods out.*

KHLUDOV. That's all there is to it? Civilian life always seemed so complicated, how people made their living was a complete mystery – perhaps it isn't so hard after all –

Turning the handle again.

GOLUBKOV. You'll look out for Serafima and take care of her if you find her, won't you?

KHLUDOV*'s too pleased with the barrel organ to hear him.*

KHLUDOV. There's nothing to it at all –

GOLUBKOV *and* CHARNOTA *leave as the delighted* KHLUDOV *keeps turning the handle of the barrel organ. Hearing the music* KRAPILIN *starts to dance. He moves slowly at first, then with increasing grace and passion.*

He dances a Cossack dance that has all of Russia in it, the Russia they're exiled from and KHLUDOV *urges him on with guttural grunts that reveal his own ache of longing.*

KRAPILIN *stamps and twirls, exalted, as the sound of honking Parisian traffic begins to drown out the barrel organ.*

End of the Sixth Dream.

Seventh Dream

The lights go up on KORZUKHIN, *in his Paris study, wearing a silk dressing gown. Pride of the place in the sumptuous apartment goes to a large safe. In civilian clothes* CAPTAIN GOLOVAN *is setting out a card table under* KORZUKHIN's *watchful gaze.*

KORZUKHIN. Monsieur Marchand m'avait averti qu'il viendra pas aujourdhui. Ne rumez pas le table. Je m'en servirai plus tard.

No response from GOLOVAN, *sullenly setting out cards and refreshments.*

Respondez vous donc quelque chose, Antoine. Don't you understand me, Antoine?

CAPTAIN GOLOVAN. No. Not really. Not at all.

KORZUKHIN. And how would one say that in French, I wonder?

CAPTAIN GOLOVAN. I wouldn't have the slightest idea.

KORZUKHIN. My dear Antoine, French is a delicate, expressive language, the language of diplomacy and love – which is just another kind of diplomacy. The Russian you cling to in Paris is good only for swearing or, God forbid, shouting revolutionary slogans. Both of which are very rude to the French who have enough braggarts and revolutionaries of their own, God knows.

You must learn French. If you don't it just makes life more difficult, it suggests a hankering for how things were, a refusal to accept the verdict of history.

What was that delightful French phrase I tried to teach you yesterday?

CAPTAIN GOLOVAN. Je . . . I'm cleaning the knives, sir.

KORZUKHIN. That would sound more like French if you put some French words into it. What's the French for knives, Antoine?

CAPTAIN GOLOVAN. It's Golovan and the word is Les Coutez.

KORZUKHIN. Excellent. I knew a man like Khludov wouldn't have had you on his staff unless you spoke French. It'll only take a little practice and it'll all come back to you.

Otherwise I might have to let you go and then what? Back to sleeping on the streets and living off kitchen scraps. And to think when we first met it was 'Yes General Khludov' and 'No General Khludov' and 'Who would you like me to hang now, General? and 'Take Korzukhin out and burn up all his furs, sir? Yes sir, I'll see to it at once, sir.'

A bell rings.

Show them in, whoever they are and take their hats and coats. They might want a game of cards. Je suis à la maison, Antoine.

He leaves and a mutinous GOLOVAN *murmurs under his breath.*

CAPTAIN GOLOVAN. The name is Golovan.

He opens the door and GOLUBKOV *stands there swaying with fatigue and hunger, footsore and weary.*

GOLUBKOV. Je vous parler à Messieur Korzukhin. Me carte –

CAPTAIN GOLOVAN. I don't need your card. It's Golubkov, isn't it?

GOLUBKOV. I remember you –

CAPTAIN GOLOVAN. The railway station – ? The Crimea – ?

GOLUBKOV. Captain Golovan? – you're working for Korzukhin now?

CAPTAIN GOLOVAN. Have you come to shoot him?

GOLUBKOV. No.

CAPTAIN GOLOVAN. That's a pity. Why not?

GOLUBKOV. Wouldn't it put you out of a job?

CAPTAIN GOLOVAN. You think I'd care?

KORZUKHIN walks in again with several decks of cards, wearing a smoking jacket and tasselled cap.

KORZUKHIN. Who is this?

GOLUBKOV. Golubkov.

KORZUKHIN. Golubkov, Golubkov, no I don't think I know any Golubkovs.

GOLUBKOV. We've met before, you probably don't recognize me. We were all on that station platform together the night Khludov burned your furs and hanged all those people.

CAPTAIN GOLOVAN. He doesn't have a hat or a coat so I'll be in the kitchen cleaning les coutez.

He leaves as a cautious KORZUKHIN *takes a closer look at* GOLUBKOV.

KORZUKHIN. The Crimea? That's in Russia, yes?

GOLUBKOV. You must remember the waiting room, how cold it was, the Reds attacking from every direction.

KORZUKHIN. The waiting room? No, no, I don't think –

GOLUBKOV. You're Paramon Korzukhin, you do remember that?

KORZUKHIN. Korzukhin, yes, that's familiar –

GOLUBKOV. You were Deputy Minister for Trade, how could you forget something like that?

KORZUKHIN. The Crimea – ? I may have passed through, yes, although I'm not admitting to anything. One had to leave Russia somehow with all those soldiers running around. Here come the Reds, here come the Whites – like a dreadful dinner party with a hostess eager to show off her wine cellar, eh? Now, however, I'm French, a naturalized citizen. Those Russian names sound so barbaric don't they? Take yours for example – Golubkov, is it? No wonder they're so hard to remember – Golubkov –

GOLUBKOV (*impatient*). Your wife is in Constantinople, living in the most dreadful poverty.

KORZUKHIN. There you go again. Wife? Constantinople? Now I really begin to think you have the wrong – Korzukhin, was it? My dear sir, I have never been on intimate terms with any Turkish woman and from what one hears, it's unlikely that any Turkish man has been, either. It looks like both of us are wasting our time. Why don't you leave, Paris has so much to offer –

GOLUBKOV. You're Korzukhin, who used to be Deputy Minister for Trade and your wife is Serafima Vladimitrovna –

KORZUKHIN (*a shake of the head*). That settles the matter.

For the past three months a Russian emigrée lady has been living here in the capacity of my personal secretary. Her charms, typing skills and accuracy in filing have so touched my heart that Mademoiselle Frejol and I are to be married at the end of the month, which would hardly be possible were I to be already married to this – what was that impossibly long name again?

GOLUBKOV. Serafima Vladimitrovna still loves you as much as any woman has ever loved a man.

KORZUKHIN. You keep saying these things –

GOLUBKOV. She's your wife.

KORZUKHIN. I think I should warn you that until we clear this confusion up any loose remarks concerning an alleged previous attachment of mine will be painful, tactless and considered a grounds for libel.

GOLUBKOV. Your wife travelled across the length of Russia sick with typhus to meet you. You were on a secret mission to General Khludov.

KORZUKHIN. Has he sent you? That idiot?

GOLUBKOV. So you remember him? What else? The frost on the windows, the dim blue lighting on the platform, the rows of bodies turning this way and that –

KORZUKHIN. The frost, yes, I remember it was unseasonably cold for the Crimea in November, such an unpleasant surprise but frost never proved anything.

Kindly touch that bell.

Complying, GOLUBKOV *rings the bell and* GOLOVAN *steps back inside the room.*

CAPTAIN GOLOVAN. Sir?

KORZUKHIN. Please confirm for this gentleman that the White Counter Intelligence has tried more than once to blackmail me over a Bolshevik spy claiming to be my wife.

CAPTAIN GOLOVAN. That's right. (*To* GOLUBKOV.) Whatever he says.

KORZUKHIN. Tell him she was last seen in the company of a suspicious character claiming to be a University student but who was clearly an agent provocateur, working for God knows whom.

CAPTAIN GOLOVAN. That's it.

GOLOVAN *leaves the room.*

GOLUBKOV. None of it happened? There was no railway station, we never met?

Stricken.

My God – did I dream it all?

Desperate.

Give me a thousand dollars and I'll make it my life's work to pay it back on any terms of interest you demand. Beggar me, work me to death but give me the money and I'll see she gets it.

KORZUKHIN. Oh dear, how very expected. Forgive my cynicism but somehow I suspected this conversation about a mythical wife was leading to a touch.

A thousand dollars? It's such an easy thing to say, isn't it? A thousand dollars, it rolls off the tongue. But before we can start to talk about a thousand dollars so casually, so effortlessly, let's think about what even one dollar means.

Pointing to the window.

Far away over there on the rooftop there burns a golden. ray – do you see it? – and beside it, high in the air with. its tail sticking up – a black cat. And what's beside it? A dollar.

He stamps his foot on the floor.

You feel that trembling, that rumbling? Down there, unimaginably deep, snake tunnels through which trains run by day and night crammed with dollars, full to bursting, endlessly thundering in the bowels of the earth.

Stands behind him, covers his eyes with his hands.

Imagine darkness and waves as high as mountains, the endless motion of the mightiest oceans, a dark beast of water that swallows men. But on that ocean with a hissing of boilers and a clanking of pistons sails a ship, a monster of the ocean itself, thrusting aside millions of gallons of water with every turn of her screws – roaring, crashing, spitting fire as it fights the waves and even there, down among the naked, sweating stokers is the monster's golden cargo, its glistening gold – like gold – dripping heart – the dollar.

Stand up!

Obediently GOLUBKOV *stands and* KORZUKHIN *takes him by the arm, steers him to the door.*

Crisis! Disaster! The Four Horsemen ready their steeds, stir in the saddle. Now – Catastrophe! There they go, all the men you passed in the street on your way here, all the men in the world marching with their heads welded into steel helmets. Now they're gathering speed, they're trotting, they're running full tilt, they're throwing themselves onto rows of barbed wire, hanging there while the guns make mincemeat of them.

Why do they do it? Because someone somewhere has offended against the Almighty Dollar. Listen! Victory! It's over! There's dancing in the streets and shouting for joy. The war is over, the dollar is avenged, long live the dollar.

Rings the bell.

Now I think you understand why it's totally impossible to hand over a sum like a thousand dollars to a total stranger.

GOLOVAN *comes in.*

GOLUBKOV. Sir?

KORZUKHIN. He's leaving. Throw him out.

CAPTAIN GOLOVAN. Leaving, throw him out, yes sir.

GOLOVAN *opens the door to reveal* CHARNOTA *standing outside in Cossack hat, wearing bright yellow underpants.*

Another visitor, sir.

KORZUKHIN. Who is it?

CAPTAIN GOLOVAN. It looks like General Charnota.

KORZUKHIN. Today seems to be Russian Day.

CHARNOTA (*walking in without being invited*). Is this him?

KORZUKHIN. It's always nice to meet somebody from the old country, but the underpants?

CHARNOTA. You don't like the colour?

KORZUKHIN. It's how you're wearing them.

CHARNOTA. I admit in a woman it would be indecent but I'm not a woman so it hardly applies, does it?

KORZUKHIN. You've been walking around Paris like that?

CHARNOTA. Of course not. I wore my trousers in the street, took them off in the hall. What do you take me for?

At GOLUBKOV.

Did he give you the money?

GOLUBKOV. Of course he didn't. There was never any chance he was going to. I was just about to leave.

CHARNOTA. It's very simple, Paramon. As a fellow Russian who risked his life fighting the Bolsheviks for you I'm asking you on this damn fool's behalf to make amends to your wife, who is living in atrocious conditions in that filthy hole

Constantinople. She's starving, living on her wits and her body and I'm sick to death of hearing Golubkov talk about it.

GOLUBKOV. It's absolutely pointless. He's even got Captain Golovan under his thumb.

KORZUKHIN. I've been racking my brains to think if any of this concerns me, but I regret that I can't –

CHARNOTA. Regrets, Paramon? Please don't say that word in my hearing. Right now, for example, I bitterly regret I didn't volunteer for the Reds when there was a chance, shoot you and everyone like you, then desert and join the Whites again.

KORZUKHIN (*to* GOLOVAN). Make a note of those remarks, Antoine.

CHARNOTA (*suddenly aware of the card table*). You like cards? What do you like to play?

KORZUKHIN. Nines.

CHARNOTA. Fancy a game?

KORZUKHIN. I only play for cash.

GOLUBKOV. We've been humiliated enough. Let's go.

CHARNOTA. Give me Khludov's medallion.

GOLUBKOV. It's all we've got left.

CHARNOTA. All you have left is Serafima.

A sigh from GOLUBKOV, *who takes the medallion out of his shoe.*

GOLUBKOV. I'm past caring, anyway.

CHARNOTA. How much?

KORZUKHIN. Ten dollars.

CHARNOTA. Excellent.

He shuffles the cards.

Nines? Very well –

Discards four cards.

Captain Golovan, bring us a plate of something. I can hardly be expected to play on an empty stomach. a steak for Golubkov and me, some sandwiches, a couple of those ripe French cheeses and a bottle or two of champagne. And some grapes, black grapes. And a pineapple. I haven't seen a pineapple since I don't know when.

CAPTAIN GOLOVAN. Certainly sir – steak, sandwiches, cheese, champagne, grapes, pineapple – *à l'instant.*

GOLUBKOV *leaves.*

CHARNOTA. Stakes?

KORZUKHIN. Ten dollars a hand.

CHARNOTA *deals two cards each and both men look at their hands.*

Card, please.

CHARNOTA *deals it face up.*

CHARNOTA. Nine.

KORZUKHIN. You win.

He flips a chip at CHARNOTA.

KORZUKHIN. Again?

CHARNOTA *deals two cards and again they look at their hands.*

KORZUKHIN. Card please.

It's dealt face up and KORZUKHIN's *lost again.*

CHARNOTA. Again?

With no hesitation KORZUKHIN *nods and the same thing happens.*

KORZUKHIN. Again.

CHARNOTA. I don't think I want to play any more.

KORZUKHIN. Another hand.

CHARNOTA. No. It's not good for you.

KORZUKHIN. Give me my cards.

CHARNOTA. If you insist.

He deals two cards and KORZUKHIN *loses again. He's breathing heavily now and nods for more cards.* CHARNOTA *slaps them onto the table and the next five hands are played like a sword fight, as they circle it, everything else forgotten.*

KORZUKHIN. Damn damn damn.

CHARNOTA. I told you this wasn't good for you.

KORZUKHIN. Another hand.

CHARNOTA. I only play for cash. You owe me eighty dollars.

KORZUKHIN. Let's play doubles.

CHARNOTA. Are you sure?

KORZKUHIN. Double the bet.

GOLUBKOV. Take the eighty, we'll manage on that.

Bearing a tray piled high with food and drink, GOLOVAN *returns.*

CAPTAIN GOLOVAN. How do you like your steaks?

CHARNOTA. Bloody for me, well done for him.

Reaching for a sandwich.

Bit of cheese, Paramon? Sandwich?

KORZUKHIN. I had lunch, thank you.

GOLOVAN *leaves.*

GOLUBKOV. Please, General –

CHARNOTA. Do you have a photograph album, Korzukhin? Prints? Picture book of erotica? Something my young friend can look at to keep him out of mischief?

KORZUKHIN. Eighty dollars? Very well. Please look away.

He goes to the safe, dials the combination and opens the door. The lights flash on and off, bells ring all over the house and GOLOVAN *rushes on with a revolver.*

KORZUKHIN. It's an anti-burglar device. It's all right, Antoine, I opened it.

Putting the gun in its holster, GOLOVAN *leaves.*

CHARNOTA. That's very impressive.

He deals and once again KORZUKHIN *loses.*

CHARNOTA. Doubles, I think we said.

KORZUKHIN. Yes – another hand.

They play four more hands, like duellists and KORZUKHIN *loses each hand. He reels away from the table.*

KORZUKHIN. I don't think I want to play any more.

CHARNOTA. I don't blame you –

He deals himself a hand, then another to an imaginary opponent, playing against himself. He checks one hand.

CHARNOTA. Another card –

He checks the other.

Nine –

Flipping the other hand over.

Damn –

He plays four more hands against himself, circling the table, responding with elation and anguish as each hand is flipped. KORZKUHIN watches him obsessively.

KORZUKHIN. How are you doing?

CHARNOTA flings more cards onto the table, rushes to the other side, runs back again.

CHARNOTA. Not now, please – .

A groan of desire and KORZUKHIN rushes to the safe, dials the combination and opens it again. Once more the lights flash, the bells ring and GOLOVAN comes in with the revolver, leaving when he sees that it's KORZUKHIN who opened the safe.

KORZUKHIN. Another hand.

CHARNOTA. Doubles?

KORZUKHIN. Yes, doubles, quickly –

CHARNOTA. The stake is one thousand five hundred and sixty dollars –

A groan from GOLUBKOV.

KORZUKHIN. Yes, yes, deal –

CHARNOTA deals and KORZUKHIN loses again.

CHARNOTA. The stake is two thousand, one hundred and twenty dollars –

KORZUKHIN. Deal – just deal –

The lights go off again and we do a time jump to later that night. When the lights come on GOLUBKOV is lying on the divan, exhausted. Music is playing distantly in another apartment. Still playing cards, CHARNOTA and KORZUKHIN's faces are lit up by the candles as they pace around the table. At last KORZUKHIN thinks he's on the verge of a winning streak although CHARNOTA has won a high pile of dollars.

KORZUKHIN. Forty thousand, nine hundred and sixty dollars.

GOLUBKOV (*anguished*). Please don't take the bet, General.

CHARNOTA. That's a very large amount of money –

GOLUBKOV. Let's go now.

CHARNOTA. That's what a bedbug would do, wouldn't it?

GOLUBKOV. I beg you –

KORZUKHIN. Well?

> CHARNOTA *deals and wins, to* KORZUKHIN*'s amazement.*

KORZUKHIN. No, it's impossible –

CHARNOTA. The bet is now eighty-one thousand nine hundred and twenty dollars –

> *With a strangled cry* KORZUKHIN *rushes to the safe again,* GOLUBKOV *covers his ears and again the lights flash, the bells ring and* GOLOVAN *comes on with the revolver – although this time he's yawning and wearing a nightshirt.*

CHARNOTA. Another hand?

> *They play,* KORZUKHIN *loses, the lights go off and rise on another time jump. Now dawn glows pinkly at the windows, the candles are burned out, there are empty champagne bottles scattered everywhere and* GOLUBKOV *sits scratching his head and yawning.*

> *The indefatigable gamblers are still circling the table, in the last stages of exhaustion.* KORZUKHIN *loses another hand, drags himself to the safe, opens it and once more the lights flash, bells sound and* GOLOVAN, *now dressed again, hurries in with the revolver.*

KORZUKHIN (*stunned*). That's it. There's no more money in the safe. And I didn't win a hand.

> *He closes the safe.*

CHARNOTA. In that case, we'll be going.

> *Stands and stretches his back.*

Would it be impolite to ask for a newspaper or large sack to carry it in?

KORZUKHIN. Antoine!

> *The yawning* GOLOVAN *comes back in, minus the revolver.*

KORZUKHIN. Do we have any sacks or newspapers on the premises? Answer carefully now.

CAPTAIN GOLOVAN. Sacks? Newspapers? No sir.

KORZUKHIN. You may go.

CAPTAIN GOLOVAN. Thank you, sir.

KORZUKHIN. Perhaps it would be better if you would take a cheque.

CHARNOTA. I'd be happy to do so if I thought any bank in Paris would pay out one million four hundred thousand dollars to a man in his underpants.

GOLUBKOV. Is that how much you won?

CHARNOTA. Give or take a few thousand dollars. My trousers, Golovan.

GOLOVAN *brings the trousers in and* CHARNOTA *ties knots in the legs of his trousers and starts stuffing the money into them.*

GOLUBKOV. Buy Khludov's medallion back. I'd like him to have it again.

CHARNOTA. How much for the medallion?

KORZUKHIN. Five hundred dollars.

CHARNOTA. Very well.

Au revoir then, Paramon – time to be going.

Rallying, KORZUKHIN *heads for the door to stop them leaving.*

KORZUKHIN. Okay, the joke's over. Give me the money back and I'll give you a thousand dollars to clear off and keep your traps shut. Clearly I'm not in the best of health. I'm not well and you took advantage of me.

CHARNOTA. I thought you were a gambling man.

KORZUKHIN. You're a pair of thieves. Antoine –

CAPTAIN GOLOVAN. Sir?

CHARNOTA (*beating* KORZUKHIN *to it*). Give me that revolver.

KORZUKHIN. Golovan! –

CAPTAIN GOLOVAN. Ici le revolveur.

He hands it across and CHARNOTA *levels it at* KORZUKHIN.

CHARNOTA. Step away from the door.

KORZUKHIN. No.

Deliberately CHARNOTA *fires wide of him.*

CHARNOTA. Just getting the feel of it.

Before he can fire a second time the bedroom door opens and LYUSKA *comes out in silk pyjamas, yawning.*

LYUSKA. What is it now?

KORZUKHIN. Some fiancée you turn out to be – fast asleep while I'm being robbed and murdered.

In shock LYUSKA *recognizes* CHARNOTA *and* GOLUBKOV. *Fortunately* KORZUKHIN's *back is to her and she's able to signal to* CHARNOTA, *begging him not to acknowledge that he knows her. As he's struggling with his reaction,* GOLUBKOV *hisses in his ear.*

GOLUBKOV. Charnota, look, it's her –

KORZUKHIN. You know Mademoiselle Frejol?

A beat as CHARNOTA *surveys her, knowing her fate is in his hands. She clasps her hands, pleads mutely with him and with a sigh he accedes.*

CHARNOTA. Frejol, Frejol – no, I don't think we know anybody of that name, do we, Golubkov?

GOLUBKOV. We don't?

Off stage we hear the dying notes of his band playing a waltz as CHARNOTA *surrenders* LYUSKA *for good.*

CHARNOTA. I knew a woman I wronged once, who did what she could for me and I drove her away – gambling did it, that should be a lesson for you, Korzukhin. But this one? – no.

LYUSKA. I thought you said only Russians spend all night drinking and playing cards and getting into fights, Paramon.

KORZUKHIN. He won over a million dollars from me and he won't give it back.

GOLUBKOV. He lost and doesn't want to pay up.

KORZUKHIN. The cards were marked.

GOLUBKOV. They were your cards.

KORZUKHIN. It's not fair – they came here in rags and now they're leaving with a fortune.

LYUSKA. You'll make another fortune. And another. You'll make as many fortunes as you need, that's what you're good at.

Antoine, show Monsieur Korzukhin to bed. And give him a stiff brandy.

KORZUKHIN. One million four hundred thousand dollars . . .

Helpless, he allows GOLOVAN *to escort him to the bedroom.*

I am not at home to any more Russians, Antoine, ever –

When he's gone, LYUSKA *turns her attention to* CHARNOTA *and* GOLUBKOV.

LYUSKA. That was a very sweet thing you did, Grisha.

CHARNOTA. Think nothing of it.

LYUSKA. I do love you, you know, but I can't go back to living like that.

CHARNOTA. I'm not asking you to.

Immediately contradicting himself.

There's no chance, then? It's all over?

Ignoring him, she turns to GOLUBKOV.

LYUSKA. How's Serafima?

GOLUBKOV. The money's for her. I don't want any of it for myself. If she can't have her husband, well, at least she can start living again.

LYUSKA. That's very sweet of you, too.

GOLUBKOV. You think so?

LYUSKA. Yes and now you can bugger off, the pair of you, no wonder I dreamt of cockroaches last night. Show up here again with or without those underpants and I'll take Golovan's gun and shoot you both. You know I'd do it, don't you?

CHARNOTA. Yes, I think you would. I think that's what attracted me to you in the first place – knowing you'd shoot me if you had to.

He snaps his heels, kisses her hand.

CHARNOTA. Au revoir, Mademoiselle Frejol. I wish you every happiness.

LYUSKA. Adieu, General. And I'm sorry I called you Madame Barabanchikova all those times.

CHARNOTA. I'm sorry I called you a whore.

LYUSKA (*at* GOLUBKOV). You still love her? That's why you're doing this?

GOLUBKOV. Yes.

LYUSKA. What a pest you are.

> CHARNOTA *swings the money stuffed trousers over his shoulder and with a derisive laugh* LYUSKA *shows them out. As she closes the door the shattered* KORZUKHIN *wanders out of the bedroom in his shirt, holding a brandy glass in his hand.*

KORZUKHIN. Have they gone?

LYUSKA. Yes, you're safe.

KORZUKHIN. Think they'll be back?

LYUSKA. No, I don't think we'll ever see them again.

KORZUKHIN. That man in his underpants – the military looking one – quite sure you've never seen him before?

LYUSKA. That man? No, not that man –

> *Sadly she closes the door and* KORZUKHIN *turns to the safe.*

KORZUKHIN. One million, four hundred thousand dollars –

> *He rushes to the safe and opens it. Once again the lights flash and the bells ring and* GOLOVAN *rushes on as we hear again the discordant chanting of the muezzins, taking us back to Constantinople.*

> *End of the Seventh Dream.*

Eighth Dream

*The cacophony becomes the steady sound of the call to prayer
from a minaret beside* KHLUDOV's *rooftop in Constantinople.
The light is strange and sinister, casting long shadows, giving the
scene an eerie quality, balanced between night and day, the East
and the West.*

Holding himself with dignity despite his ragged clothing,
KHLUDOV *is talking to* KRAPILIN, *still there but now invisible
even to* KHLUDOV.

KHLUDOV. How did you do it? What makes you so special? Out
of all the hundreds I hung, the ones who died cursing me, the
ones whose eyes saw me last of all of anything in their lives –
why you? And how?

Who would have thought that Krapilin of all people would
have been the one to work the trick, to escape from that line of
faint blue light, climb down from his lamp post?

I've hung professors, mystics, chemistry teachers, some of the
best and cleverest men and women in Russia but none of them
managed to pull it off.

Slicing a piece of salami.

When you think about it, what a ridiculous waste of time and
effort it all was. If I hadn't hanged one person the Bolsheviks
would still have beaten us. And then what? I'd probably still
have ended up here, dying of the heat and boredom. And where
would you have been? Probably somewhere you'd be no better
off, no happier, no more miserable.

Unseen by him, SERAFIMA *enters, watches and listens.*

You're dead, Tikhi's dead, all those moons, all those lamp
posts – there are living people who need me now, do you
understand?

SERAFIMA (*gently*). You're doing it again. Talking to yourself.

KHLUDOV. Lots of Generals talk to themselves. It's a lonely life,
command. If you don't like it, why do you stay?

SERAFIMA. Because after Golubkov left you dragged me out
of the Grand Bazaar by my hair and threatened to shoot me if
I went there again. Because there's something wrong with you

and you've no one to take care of you and if anything happens to you there's no one to take care of me.

KHLUDOV. I'm sick, aren't I?

SERAFIMA. Very sick.

Cutting a slice of salami for her.

KHLUDOV. I hear you moving about in that room next to mine. I keep listening for the sounds you make. Do you mind that?

SERAFIMA. I don't know. I don't think so.

KHLUDOV. I hear you getting up. I say to myself – now she's out of bed. Now she's dressing. Now she's looking at herself in the mirror. (*Abruptly.*) Any news from Golubkov?

SERAFIMA. No.

KHLUDOV. When he comes back, if he comes back, we'll all have to go our different ways again.

SERAFIMA. Do you think they're dead?

KHLUDOV. Yes, I should think the pair of them have had their throats cut somewhere between here and France.

SERAFIMA (*blinking back tears*). I can't believe I let him go. It was just so humiliating to be caught like that, with that Greek and a basket of shopping.

KHLUDOV. Many an Archduchess has sold herself for less.

A sigh.

Yes, I'll find some way of getting back and 'I'm Khludov', I shall say, 'I've come back, you see, General Roman Khludov, the Butcher of the Crimea at your service'.

SERAFIMA. You'll use your own name?

KHLUDOV. I quite like my name.

SERAFIMA. They'll shoot you.

KHLUDOV. Probably. Snow. Greatcoats. A cellar.

Barking a short laugh.

I did some terrible things, dreadful things and although I like to think I did them with style, with a certain amount of panache and now and again, it, may be, wit –

A shrug.

Well, I may be mad but I'm not a cockroach and I don't intend to scuttle around in the dark until I fall off the kitchen table.

The muezzin once again makes the call to prayer. When the last notes have died away, through the door that leads to the roof come GOLUBKOV *and* CHARNOTA, *wearing new suits,* CHARNOTA *carrying a silver topped cane and expensive leather luggage.*

SERAFIMA. Sergei –

GOLUBKOV. Serafima –

They stare at each other, fighting for words. KHLUDOV *masters his jealousy, clears his throat.*

KHLUDOV. How was Paris?

CHARNOTA. It was very – Parisian, that's the only word for it.

SERAFIMA *stares at* GOLUBKOV.

SERAFIMA. I waited for you.

GOLUBKOV. It's quite gone out of my head what I was going to say if you were still here.

SERAFIMA. I've been to the harbour every day thinking you might be coming back by ship, then I get scared that you might be at the Railway Station so I hurry there and then I think No, he'll walk if he has to, so I go to one of the city gates only I hear a ship's siren and I rush back to the harbour and halfway there I think What if he's lying in a street in Paris, starving? –

KHLUDOV (*controlling his jealousy again*). You saw Korzukhin?

GOLUBKOV (*nodding his head, eyes only for* SERAFIMA). He's completely given you up, you know.

SERAFIMA. Then congratulate me, Sergei – I'm a widow.

KHLUDOV. I thought you'd stay there. In Paris.

CHARNOTA. So did I, yes. But here I am, back in this filthy hole.

SERAFIMA *and* GOLUBKOV *throw themselves at each other, passionately embracing.* KHLUDOV *averts his eyes.*

KHLUDOV. A charming picture. Any news of Lyuska?

CHARNOTA. No.

KHLUDOV. She'll be back.

CHARNOTA. I don't think so.

KHLUDOV (*vaguely*). Well, let me know how it all works out.

He reaches into the barrel organ and pulls out a small suitcase.

I'm off.

CHARNOTA. Where are you going?

SERAFIMA. He's going back to Russia. He says he doesn't care if they shoot him or not.

KHLUDOV. Well, General Charnota? What about it?

CHARNOTA (*tempted*). I've never run away from anything, but running to certain death and torture? What if they don't kill you straight away?

KHLUDOV. Torture, no, that wouldn't be funny but to live like this, not even to be a soldier any more – to starve to death here –

CHARNOTA. I won almost one and a half million dollars off Korzukhin at cards.

KHLUDOV. Put it away.

SERAFIMA (*surprised*). He doesn't play cards. He's never played cards. He's too mean.

Making up his mind for good, KHLUDOV *snaps an order at the invisible* KRAPILIN.

KHLUDOV. Fall in.

(*To* CHARNOTA.) Can't make you change your mind? Pity. There's something about a ship, don't you find? The engine throbbing away, the little birds on the mast –

What was that tune you were always playing?

Without waiting for an answer he leads the invisible KRAPILIN *away, humming the waltz the brass band always played. He holds the door open for* KRAPILIN *to exit, then he's gone, too.*

CHARNOTA *opens one of the suitcases and takes a handful of dollars out.*

CHARNOTA. Half for you and half for me, Sergei. That's what we said, didn't we?

GOLUBKOV. Give all mine to Serafima. I don't want any of it.

Damn – I forgot to give Khludov his medallion back.

SERAFIMA. I don't want his money. I want to do what he's doing. I want to go back to Russia.

CHARNOTA. You want to put your head in the noose, too? (*To* GOLUBKOV.) Tell her she's crazy.

GOLUBKOV. She's right. You're right, Serafima. It's what I want. I want to go back. It's all I ever wanted.

CHARNOTA. The very best of luck to you. I'll keep it all. You're sure? Both of you?

SERAFIMA. I'm sure, Sergei, aren't you?

GOLUBKOV. I'd like to go tonight. Before we die of the heat and the noise.

SERAFIMA. Were we dreaming these past months, Sergei? Where were we running from? What did we think we were running to? Were there really all those hanged men on the station platform?

We hear a steam train thundering through the night, whistle shrieking. More trains sound and we hear CHARNOTA's *brass band playing the waltz, the honking traffic in Parisian streets, the alarm bells from* KORZUKHIN's *apartment and finally the notes of the* MONKS *chanting the Liturgy from the first moments of the play.*

When it dies away the Muezzin sounds again and then a clock strikes offstage and we hear YANKO YANKOVICH's *voice in the distance.*

YANKO YANKOVICH (*voice only*). Messieurs, mesdames, les courses commencent. The favourite sport of the Russian Tsars, never before seen outside the walls of the Imperial palaces –

SERAFIMA *shakes her head, her mind made up.*

SERAFIMA. I want to see the Nevsky again, I want to feel cold, I want to see snow, I want to forget everything that's happened.

GOLUBKOV. None of it happened. We imagined it all. In a month we'll be home and it'll start snowing and the snow will cover everything, our footsteps, everything.

Taking her hand.

Come on. We're leaving.

SERAFIMA. No more dreams.

They rush off, leaving CHARNOTA *alone, holding the money. He calls to* YANKO.

CHARNOTA. What's the outsider in the first race?

ATHANASIUS' *voice answers.*

ATHANASIUS. Shooting star at eighty to one.

CHARNOTA *pulls all the money out of the suitcase.*

CHARNOTA. One million, four hundred thousand on Shooting Star – to win –

He throws it in the air and we snap to a blackout.

End of the Eighth Dream.

End.